Fantasy Football (and Baseball)

for Smart People:

How to Turn Your Hobby

into a Fortune

DraftKings.com was instrumental in the creation of this book. I've partnered with them on this special 100 percent deposit bonus for new users. Deposit money and they double it. Just visit DraftKings.com/Bales to sign up.

Fantasy Football (and Baseball) for Smart People:
How to Turn Your Hobby into a Fortune

Table of Contents

4 You Down With GPPS!? How to Win Tournaments

- How to increase upside to win big tournaments
- Why you need to pair a QB with his receivers
- Why everything you think you know about fantasy baseball strategy is wrong
- Understanding tournament variance
- How a contrarian tournament strategy can lead to big success

5 The Final Piece of the Puzzle: Creating Projections and Lineups

- The stats that matter when projecting players
- How to turn projections into values to build lineups
- NFL and MLB walkthroughs from daily fantasy's most profitable players
- Site-specific strategies to win cash

6 Getting Analytical: An Appendix of Extra Data

- Data on paying for pitching over hitting, how wind speed affects NFL stats, and more

7 A Sample from *How to Cash in on the Future of the Game*

- Short sample on money management from my first daily fantasy book

    Postface

I Preface

For the past decade, I've pretty much kicked ass at fantasy sports. Fantasy football is my bread-and-butter; in my heyday—and by 'heyday' I mean last year—I participated in so many fantasy football leagues that I'm actually embarrassed to admit it the number.

It was 36.

Ah, that wasn't so bad. I actually ended up winning around half of those leagues, which is pretty much mathematically impossible by luck alone. I'm not really bragging since my success is the result of being a complete loser who runs Monte Carlo simulations in his free time, but I figured other people were interested in being fantasy losers, too, so I started the *Fantasy Football for Smart People* book series.

With my season-long fantasy experience, I figured I should try to make money by dabbling in daily fantasy sports—one-day fantasy contests with real cash prizes. They're like an entire fantasy season condensed into 24 hours, which has a ton of advantages.

When I first started playing daily fantasy sports, I figured I'd run over people using my traditional fantasy knowledge. Not so. I got killed, actually. There are a whole lot of similarities between season-long and daily fantasy leagues, but there are some major differences, too.

As I began to play more and learn the tricks of the trade, I met some of the game's pros—the top players who are long-term winners. It's always tough to calculate how much money these guys are actually netting after accounting for losses and the commission taken by each daily fantasy site, but there's pretty good evidence that some of these guys are profiting tens of thousands of dollars a week.

Let that sink in.

And that's really why daily fantasy sports are the wave of the future. Yes, you don't have to deal with injuries or give up on a team with a 1-5 record come Week 7 of the NFL season, but the main advantage—the primary benefit offered by daily fantasy sports—is profitability. You can make money playing the game, and you can make lots of it.

I set out to determine how the top players are winning all of this cash. I wanted to figure out why I kept seeing the same names winning all of the tournaments. So I worked with a few of them on my first book in the world of daily fantasy sports—*Fantasy Football for Smart People: How to Cash in on the Future of the Game*. I uncovered more information than I could squeeze into a single paperback.

And even since I published that book just a few short months ago, the daily fantasy industry has grown exponentially. To fully grasp the development, consider that the highest grand prize ever handed out in daily fantasy went to 'CSUMRAM88'—Peter Jennings, who helped immensely in writing my first book—and it was $150,000.

Not a bad payday. But fast-forward one year, and three daily fantasy sites are set to hand out grand prizes of $1 million. That's over six times the highest-ever prize handed out just 12 months prior!

One of the frontrunners in the industry is DraftKings. Their "Millionaire Grand Final" has a record $3.1 million in prizes. That's enough money to buy 103 new 2014 Mercedes CLA-Class cars. Or 52 Princess Diana beanie babies. Your choice.

With all of the new users playing daily fantasy, the opportunity to make money is unbelievable. The more novices, the greater the pool of users who can potentially be profitable.

But you aren't going to just jump right into daily fantasy sports and be a long-term winner right out of the gate. Although you can put as little or as much time into the game as you'd like, the best players are always increasing their win probability to optimize their expected return. They employ little tricks regarding money management, league selection, player projections, and so on, all in an effort to increase their win rate by a few percentage points.

In the world of daily fantasy sports, the difference between a beginner and a pro isn't quite as wide of a gap as you might think. So the goal of this book is to show you how to do everything in your power to ensure you come out on top over the long-run.

Understanding Variance

One of the most important aspects of playing daily fantasy sports—or participating in any marketplace setting, for that matter—is understanding variance. No matter what you do, you can never *guarantee* victory. That's vital to not only comprehend, but also to account for in all of your fantasy-related decisions. Daily fantasy sports have an element of randomness; if you create teams or enter leagues as though they don't—as if you know what will transpire beyond a shadow of a doubt—you're going to go bankrupt.

In short, you need to account for your own fallibility. No matter how much work you put into daily fantasy, sometimes you're just going to be wrong. Even worse, sometimes you'll be right—you'll optimize your win probability and do everything needed to win—and you'll still lose. That sucks.

But you need to be prepared for it. All of your actions need to be governed by a sound understanding of risk and reward. When is it okay to be aggressive? When should you play it conservatively? How should variance affect your decisions?

There's zero doubt that daily fantasy sports, although possessing a component of luck, are games of skill. I'm going to help you figure out how to become a more skillful player so that you can transform into one of the game's profitable players.

A Two-Sport Approach

This book is going to concentrate on football and baseball. I decided to take a two-sport approach because I think it's a great way to show how the most foundational daily fantasy rules can and should be applied across sports.

Regardless of the sport you're playing, the basic concepts that are accepted by daily fantasy's pros remain consistent. You need to properly manage your money. You need to create player values that compare expected production to salary. You need to structure your lineups in a manner that reflects your league type.

There are differences, too. I've worked with a few of daily fantasy's top players—most notably Mike5754, CSURAM88, naapstermaan, Notorious, headchopper, and stlcardinals84—to provide you with advice that's both meaningful and actionable. In applying the game's core concepts to two sports and then exploring the effects in greater detail, I hope to successfully fuse the big picture with important specifics in a way that will be useful to you when you sit down to play daily fantasy sports.

I get by with a little help from my friends

I just re-watched "The Wonder Years" series on Netflix with my girlfriend (by the way, yes, it's more than a little shocking that I have a girlfriend—a good one, too—considering the amount of time I spend on fantasy sports). That doesn't really have much to do with this book, but I wanted to justify the title of this heading.

Anyway, in addition to all of the friends I've made as I transition more heavily into the daily fantasy industry, I'm also getting by with (more than) a little help from my friends at DraftKings when it comes to writing this book.

I started playing at DraftKings in 2012 and it quickly become my site of choice. I approached them about working together on this book and asked them an important question: can I use your data to determine the best strategies in daily fantasy? Thankfully, they said yes.

One of the ways I hope that this book differentiates itself from my first daily fantasy book (in addition to the MLB content) is that data. Working with DraftKings, I'm going to give you guys some data on *what's actually working* in daily fantasy.

Should you pair a quarterback and a wide receiver? Should the majority of your hitters be from the same team? How can you really increase your team's ceiling? What's the best 50/50 strategy? No more guessing. It's time for hard data on what's winning.

As a disclaimer, please note that I didn't get access to DraftKings' database, I never analyzed any specific lineups, and I have no idea how certain users structured their teams. I actually don't care about that stuff, either; I think analyzing winning lineups as a whole has way more practical value than trying to pick apart what a single player did in one specific instance. All of the information to which I had access was supplied by DraftKings upon my request, and it's all located in this book. And trust me, it's good stuff.

In addition to their data, I think it will be cool to use DraftKings as a template on how to actually play and win at a single site. So instead of figuring it out on your own, I'll show you how to mold the principles from this book into a useful, site-specific strategy.

A Daily Fantasy Glossary

As I began writing this book, I realized there's a whole bunch of terminology specific to the daily fantasy realm that's not used among season-long fantasy owners. I use a lot of these terms throughout the book, so I've created a glossary to which you can refer if you're unsure what the hell I'm talking about.

+EV

Positive Expected Value; a situation in which you expect a positive return on your investment. Daily fantasy players are constantly searching for +EV situations.

$/Point

Dollars per point; the number of dollars you must spend (in cap space) for every point a player is projected to score. A lower $/point is preferable.

50/50

A league type in which the top half of all entrants get paid and the bottom half lose their entry fee. 50/50 leagues are generally considered safe, but they can become dangerous if you enter the same lineup into multiple leagues.

Bankroll

The amount of money you're willing to invest in daily fantasy sports

Bearish

A pessimistic outlook on a particular player, team, or situation. If you're bearish on a player, you wouldn't use him in your lineups.

Bullish

The opposite of bearish; an optimistic outlook on a particular situation. If you're bullish on a player, you'd use him in your daily fantasy lineups.

Buy-In

The amount of money needed to enter a particular league

Ceiling

A player, team, or lineup's upside; the maximum number of points they could score

Commission

The fee charged by the daily fantasy sites to play in a league; typically around 10 percent of the total buy-ins

DFS
Acronym for daily fantasy sports

Exposure
The amount of money invested in a player; if you have a lot of exposure to a particular player, it means you have a relatively high percentage of your bankroll placed on him.

Fade
To avoid a particular player or game, i.e. "I'm fading the Patriots game because there are 30 MPH winds."

Floor
A player, team, or lineup's downside; the minimum number of points they could score

Freeroll
A daily fantasy league that's free to enter but has cash prizes

GPP
"Guaranteed Prize Pool"; a league in which the prize is guaranteed, regardless of the number of entrants

Head-to-head (Heads-Up)
A one-one-one daily fantasy league

Hedge
Actions taken to reduce the overall risk of your lineups; if you're excessively bullish on a particular lineup, for example, you would hedge by creating other lineups without any of the same players, even if it's sub-optimal. When you hedge, you're reducing risk at the cost of also reducing upside.

High-Low

Also known as "stars and scrubs"; when you select multiple elite, high-salary players to accompany low-priced, bargain bin players (in contrast to a balanced strategy)

Multiplier

A league in which you can multiply your entry fee by a certain factor based on the payouts; in a 5x multiplier, for example, the winners get paid out five times their entry fee. The higher the multiplier, the more high-risk/high-reward the league.

Overlay

When a daily fantasy site loses money on a GPP; if $20,000 is guaranteed but there are only $18,000 worth of entrants, the overlay is $2,000.

PPR

Point per reception; a scoring system that provides a point for all catches and dramatically influences strategy

Qualifier

A league in which the winners don't receive cash, but rather win a "ticket" into another league; a 10-team qualifier with an $11 buy-in might give away one ticket into a larger league with a $100 buy-in, for example; in opposition to cash games

Reach

To select a player who doesn't provide great value, i.e. a high $/point; reaches typically result in -EV (negative expected value) situations

ROI

Return on Investment

Stacking

To pair multiple players from the same professional team in an effort to increase upside; stacking is particularly popular in daily fantasy baseball

The 10 Laws

As I did in my first daily fantasy book, I'll end each chapter with "The 10 Laws." These will be 10 specific, actionable nuggets of information—pragmatic versions of more complex ideas—that will aid you in your quest for daily fantasy sports dominance.

Regardless of the sports you play or your daily fantasy goals, my hope is that *Fantasy Football (and Baseball) for Smart People: How to Turn Your Hobby into a Fortune* will be enlightening and helpful in your journey. Thanks for the support, and let's go win some money!

1 Back to School: Building a Research Foundation

"If we knew what it was we were doing, it wouldn't be called research, would it?"

- *Albert Einstein*

When I first started playing daily fantasy sports, I thought I could use general sports knowledge to run over opponents. That wasn't the case, and it highlighted the idea that a vast understanding of sports alone isn't going to magically turn you into a long-term winner in daily fantasy.

You need to do research. That doesn't necessarily mean spending countless hours creating projections and running simulations, but so much of daily fantasy sports is about obtaining as much up-to-date information as possible. Who is starting for the Royals tonight? What's the weather like in San Francisco? How has Matt Holliday performed in his past five games?

Even the world's brightest sports minds need to examine each situation—every lineup, every game, every player—in isolation. That means building a foundation of research through which you can collect relevant information as quickly and painlessly as possible.

There's so much awesome data and analysis out there these days that it can sometimes paradoxically make the research process more difficult. It's not uncommon for a novice daily fantasy player to get into the game and become overwhelmed with questions of "Well where in the hell am I supposed to start?"

There are so many fantastic sports and fantasy sports resources available, many of which can help you regardless of the sport you're looking to play. So before diving into some sport-specific sites, let's examine some broader sources of information that should be a staple of your daily fantasy research foundation.

Vegas

There's a huge difference between sportsbetting and daily fantasy sports. The latter game pits you against another person like yourself (instead of a sportsbook), meaning daily fantasy sports outcomes are governed by skill. But when playing daily fantasy, you can and should utilize the work done in Vegas whenever possible.

The reason? The Vegas sharps and their sophisticated computers create really, really accurate lines. There seems to be a prevailing notion that books generate lines to create equal action on both sides of a potential bet, but that's not the case. Vegas used to utilize public opinion as a stronger factor in their lines, but most bettors are too advanced these days for Vegas to do that.

So for the most part, Vegas cares about getting their lines correct. If they post weak lines, the sharks are going to kill them. Even amateurs have become much sharper with their bets; they're now like trout instead of guppies.

Any time you can use the research of others who are trustworthy, you should do it. It's the fastest and most accurate way to approach daily fantasy sports research, projections, and lineup creation.

I'm going to discuss more about how to utilize Vegas's lines down the road, but they're directly applicable to every sport. You can and should target players in games that Vegas predicts to be high-scoring, for example. You can use Vegas to project touchdowns, runs scored, and so on.

Vegas even puts out player props with their best guesses for individual player stats. When Vegas projects the Patriots at 28 points and tight end Rob Gronkowski with an over/under of 6.5 catches, 90.5 yards, and 0.5 touchdowns at (-150), that information means something.

So forget what your mom and teachers told you. Not only is copying a good thing, but it's probably the *best* way to quickly formulate really accurate predictions.

Fantasy Pros

Regardless of the sports you play, FantasyPros.com needs to be a mainstay in your daily fantasy research arsenal. Fantasy Pros has all sorts of unique information, the majority of which is the result of independently generated expert projections and rankings.

Fantasy Pros allows experts from various sites to upload their projections (for both season-long and daily fantasy sports). I'm one of those experts, and I can tell you that there's a real incentive to posting quality projections because Fantasy Pros ranks all of the experts. There's no motivation quite like showing users you know your shit.

So Fantasy Pros is basically one big database of aggregate expert opinions—a "wisdom of the crowd" approach to fantasy sports. That method is incredibly valuable and the one through which I have found the most success in making predictions of all types in the past.

The Value of Aggregate Data

Let me give you an example of how aggregate data can be useful. Prior to the 2013 fantasy football season, I was incredibly down on Seahawks running back Marshawn Lynch. I saw Lynch as an aging running back coming off of a career year (and thus likely to regress) who was also situation-dependent—unlikely to provide meaningful contributions if Seattle were to get down in games.

I still think I made some fair points regarding Lynch, although I turned out to be at least somewhat wrong on him. But even though I had Lynch ranked outside of my top 15 running backs in 2013, I still drafted him not once, but twice. I disregarded my rankings to scoop him up in the second round of two drafts, and those two squads ended up as a couple of my best on the season.

Here's why I drafted Lynch, despite my projections, and the reason that aggregate data can be so useful: it's crucial to account for your own fallibility. I'm supposedly a fantasy expert writing a book that's supposed to be a guide for your daily fantasy sports efforts, and I'm telling you that I'm wrong. I'm wrong *a lot*.

Now, hopefully I'm right a lot, too—enough that I (and you) see a sustainable long-term advantage. But it would be a mistake to think that I'll always be right, and an even bigger flaw to not account for my own weaknesses in my projections and all other fantasy sports-related decisions.

And that's really what aggregate data helps us do; it aids us in limiting the impact of our biases. I was so down on Lynch prior to 2013 that it just didn't make much sense to think that I was going to be right over literally hundreds of other fantasy experts. It's one thing to believe in your own abilities, and it's another altogether to blindly overlook the independent research of many other experts—the equivalent of closing your eyes, covering your ears, and yelling "nuh-uh, nuh-uh."

The most important part about a "wisdom of the crowd" approach to daily fantasy sports? It works. Over time, it's going to be really difficult for individuals to beat the consensus, assuming 1) "the consensus" is made up of experts in a field and 2) there's no "groupthink", i.e. they reached their opinions independently of one another. If those two conditions are met, the consensus will beat the majority of individuals over the long run.

Fantasy Pros Tools

All of Fantasy Pros' tool are built around independent expert opinions. You can check out aggregate daily or weekly rankings for any sport to see where experts stand on each player. Fantasy Pros also has a salary cap analysis tool that imports salary data from various sites and combines the data with the expert-generated projections to create value reports for each position.

Further, you can handpick the expert opinions you'd like to consider. Think that I make projections so horrific that it's a wonder Fantasy Pros would even let me on their site? No problem, just remove "Jonathan Bales" from the data sample and you're good to go (big mistake).

You don't need to (nor should you) use the data at Fantasy Pros as a standalone when creating daily fantasy lineups, but the aggregate approach, when combined with Vegas and other research tools, can be extremely valuable.

RotoGrinders

Dedicated solely to daily fantasy sports, RotoGrinders.com is the destination for the majority of the game's best players.

There's endless information in the form of podcasts, Google Hangouts, articles, forums, projections, and a daily fantasy "school" on which I work called GrindersU. GrindersU actually makes for an outstanding supplement to this book.

The primary value of RotoGrinders is that it brings all sorts of data to your front door. In the NFL research section, for example, there are tools that contain player stats, targets, consistency metrics, a salary "market watch," Vegas lines and props, defense vs. position data, snap counts, downloadable site salaries, and more. In their MLB research section, you can access player splits, weather data, lineup information, advanced Sabermetrics, ballpark factors, closer charts, site scoring comparisons, etc.

Ultimately, RotoGrinders brings together all of the research you need to do to become a long-term winner. The site should be part of the crux of your daily fantasy plan of attack.

DraftKings' Playbook

With daily fantasy is still in its infancy, there are very few places where you can get not only daily-specific analysis, but also site-specific content. Well, DraftKings is revamping their blog (called Playbook), and I'm going to be helping to lead the charge.

The primary advantage? Like I said, DraftKings is providing me (and you) with unprecedented access to their game data. In addition to everything you'll find in this book, I'll be using actual DraftKings game histories to generate actionable advice on their blog. It's an awesome and unique situation that can really benefit you in your effort to master a daily fantasy site.

Twitter

When Twitter first came out, I remember telling people "well that's a dumb idea." Fast-forward to today and Twitter is the present and future of breaking news.

For daily fantasy players, Twitter can be an extremely useful tool. There's no better and faster way to uncover player news than directly from the beat writers who cover the teams. On Twitter, you can quickly create a list of relevant writers and analysts who, although their opinions might be wacky, provide invaluable information regarding injuries, potential game plans, and late lineup changes.

Knowing What's Important

Before jumping into some sport-specific research options, I want to mention that it's easy to become inundated with data when doing research. It eventually all comes down to numbers. But which numbers are we to accept?

Take this example. Prince Fielder is hitting .345 over his last five games, but he's facing a lefty, against which he has a .267 career average. He also has just a .714 OPS (On-Base Plus

Slugging) and an uncanny .700 BABIP (Batting Average on Balls In Play) over the past week.

If you have no idea what any of that means, don't worry. The point is that there are all kinds of numbers available, especially in a sport like baseball, so analyzing all of them can seem like an insurmountable task.

I'll discuss which stats are most important in each sport, but the fundamental concept to understand is that we're always on the lookout for stats that are predictive. If it can't help us predict the future, it's not going to do us much good in fantasy sports.

Final NFL box scores are an example of that. There are all sorts of stats out there that show running is correlated with winning: Team X is 45-1 when they run the ball 30 times, or something to that effect.

But that's not going to help you predict future wins because running the ball is typically an *effect* of winning, not a *cause* of it. Teams run the ball late in games when they have a lead, creating the illusion that balance is suitable. If you look at just first half stats, though, you'll see that the best teams are those that pass the ball efficiently.

That's why a stat like Adjusted Net YPA is much more valuable; it's predictive, whereas rushing attempts are simply explanatory. If you're going to pick NFL winners based on how many times you think they'll run the ball, you're going to be in big trouble.

In the case of Fielder, considering only his batting average might lead you astray. His other numbers suggest that he's not hitting the ball that well (the low OPS) and that he's getting lucky to accumulate hits (.700 BABIP). In that example, Fielder's OPS and BABIP are more predictive than his batting average, and thus possess more practical value.

If OPS and BABIP scare you, you're not alone. Not everyone stays in on Friday nights to update their Excel spreadsheets (don't judge). So if you find yourself in that crowd, just know that you don't need to understand a million different stats to play daily fantasy sports; you just need to understand which ones can help you make better predictions.

NFL-Specific Research

When I first began writing about the NFL, I got into film study pretty heavily. Quickly, though, I realized the limitations of blindly studying film; namely; it's difficult to obtain objective insights, it doesn't scale, and there are questions regarding its ability to evolve and improve.

So I turned to analytics. Now, if you want to know how often NFL offenses convert on fourth-and-whatever, when teams should go for two, or how frequently they should pass on first down given the score, I probably know the answer.

But there are limitations to "blind" analytics, too. The NFL is a unique animal in that, unlike the NBA or MLB, it's really difficult to standardize. Baseball in particular is an extremely binary sport; you have a batter and a hitter, and there are only a limited number of events that can transpire. Because of that standardization, the numbers have a lot of meaning; for the most part, a strikeout is a strikeout, while in football, an event like an interception might not even be the fault of the quarterback.

Another reason that NFL analytics aren't quite as trustworthy as those in baseball is that the teams play just once a week. That creates 1) sample size issues and 2) questions regarding whether or not players can truly "get hot."

In baseball, players go through hot and cold streaks all of the time. That's made possible when you play every night. In the NFL, however, "momentum" on a week-to-week basis is really difficult to sustain. Yes, some teams and players appear to get hot and cold, but the steaks are actually very close to what we'd expect in a completely random environment.

Further, with only 16 games, it's really difficult to judge players in the NFL. We'd never do that over the same sample in baseball because it would represent less than 10 percent of the games in that season.

All in all, there's more predictability in baseball than football (over the course of their respective seasons). Football is a situation-specific sport in which no two plays ever really resemble one another, and luck plays a larger role than most of us would like to admit.

But here's the good news: randomness is our friend.

Why Randomness Can Be Profitable

You're playing poker and you manage to land a Royal Flush—an event that occurs once in every 649,739 hands. Nice work. What's the probability that your next five-card hand is worse than that one?

The answer is 99.99985 percent.

Even though the distribution of cards would be random, you could effectively bet everything you own that your next hand will be worse than a Royal Flush. That's because the previous hand was an outlier—a data point far from the median.

When it comes down to it, much of daily fantasy football is about identifying outliers and then "guessing" that they'll regress toward the mean (or the median). That's made possible because of the relatively high level of randomness inherent to football.

This is a really important point, so let's take a look at a section on randomness from my first book *Fantasy Football for Smart People: How to Dominate Your Draft:*

> *Back in 2008, I had running back Thomas Jones ranked well ahead of most owners. Jones was playing for the Jets and coming off a season in which he ran for 1,119 yards, but averaged just 3.6 yards-per-rush and scored only two total touchdowns. Those two scores represented just 0.59 percent of Jones' 338 touches in 2007.*

ESPN had Jones ranked 21st among all running backs. I had him 10th. Why would I possibly rank a running back coming off a season in which he tallied 3.6 yards-per-carry and two total touchdowns in my top 10? Regression toward the mean.

Regression toward the mean is a phenomenon wherein "extreme" results tend to end up closer to the average on subsequent measurements. That is, a running back who garners 338 touches and scores only twice is far more likely to improve upon that performance than one who scored 25 touchdowns.

0-16 Detroit Lions: A Coach's Dream?

Regression toward the mean is the reason the NFL coaches who take over the worst teams are in a far superior position to those who take over quality squads. If I were an NFL coach, there is no team I would prefer to take over more than the 2008 Detroit Lions. Coming off of an 0-16 season, the Lions were almost assured improvement in 2009 simply because everything went wrong the previous season. Even though Detroit was a bad team, any coach who took over in 2009 was basically guaranteed to oversee improvement in following years.

This same sort of logic it the reason there are so many first-round "busts" in fantasy football. Players almost always get selected in the first round because they had monster years in the prior season. In effect, most first-rounders are the "outliers" from the prior season's data, and their play is more likely to regress than improve in the current year. It isn't that these players are poor picks, but rather the combination of quality play, health, and other random factors that led to their prior success is unlikely to work out so fortunately again.

Players Aren't "Due"

Walk into any casino in America and you will see lines of hopeful grandmothers behind slot machines that haven't paid recently. Since the machines pay a specific average of money over the course of their lives and these numbers always even out over the long run, surely an underperforming slot machine must be due to pay out soon, right?

This is one of the biggest misconceptions regarding statistics and regression, and it is the cause of millions of lost dollars each year. In a set of random data, previous occurrences have absolutely no effect on future events. If you flip a coin right now and it lands on heads, the probability that it lands on heads again on your next flip is still 50 percent.

Similarly, if the overall payout rate of a slot machine is 40 percent, the most likely outcome of placing $1,000 into it is walking away with $400. You could walk away big or you (theoretically) could lose every penny, but the most probable single dollar amount you could "win" is $400. So when the previous 100 pulls of the lever are fruitless, the payout *"improvement" that is likely to take place over the next 100 pulls isn't because the machine is "due," but rather it is simply working as normal.*

Utilizing Randomness in Daily Fantasy Football

I'm discussing randomness in the "NFL-specific" section of this chapter because football has proven again and again to be a more random game than baseball. That doesn't make it less predictable because, as I've shown, randomness can paradoxically be extremely predictable (thus allowing for daily fantasy football to be a highly skillful game).

All we need to do is identify the outliers. When a stud running back starts the season with just 100 total yards in his first three games, his salary will likely drop on the daily fantasy sites. It's also probably an outstanding time to "buy low" on him because, in a sport in which the majority of what we perceive as momentum is likely illusory, there's a high probability that his future production will exceed his current cost.

In MLB, however, players are far more susceptible to streaky play. If a star outfielder starts the season 0-for-14 in his first three games, it's probably smart to fade him, as he could very well already be in a slump. He's not nearly as likely to produce as the running back coming off of three poor performances since his play one day is strongly linked to his performance in the next. No such causal relationship exists in the NFL, at least not to the same extent.

Much of daily fantasy football is about identifying randomness and realizing that it will regress toward the mean. Daily fantasy baseball, on the other hand, is more about recognizing trends, both in the long-term and the near future, and understanding that they're more likely to continue. It's an important distinction to understand.

Football Outsiders

FootballOutsiders.com is an extremely popular NFL stats site that, although not fantasy-specific, offers a plethora of unique information that can be useful to fantasy owners. One of their proprietary stats is DVOA—a metric that measures offensive and defensive output independently of the opponent.

Such a stat can be of use to daily fantasy owners searching for the "true" strength of a defense. It's especially useful early in the season when typical bulk stats like yards or touchdowns allowed are influenced strongly by 1) opponent strength and 2) a small sample.

One of my personal favorite FO stats is "Adjusted Line Yards." ALY separates running back production from offensive line play. It's an awesome stat to use when assessing backup running backs because it can tell you how much of the starter's success is due to his own talent versus that of his offensive line.

Pro Football Focus

ProFootballFocus.com was one of the first sites—and still one of the only sites—to mold film study with analytics. They break down every play in every game, grading players on a variety of factors.

While you can debate the value of their subjective grading, PFF offers a number of objective insights that are of incredible value: stats like time spent in the pocket, yards after contact per rush, average depth of targets, performance in the slot, yards per route run, and so on. All of the unique stats can help identify and separate the signal from the noise.

Prior to each NFL week, I visit PFF to analyze cornerback stats. In the same way that you should select hitters based on the quality of the pitcher they'll be facing, there's lots of value in targeting wide receivers who will go head-to-head against a struggling cornerback.

4for4

4for4.com is a season-long fantasy football site that provides all kinds of data and analysis that's useful in the daily realm. Some of their beneficial stats includes schedule-adjusted analysis, consistency data, and situational stats. They also provide DraftKings-specific value reports that can be used to generate aggregate rankings.

rotoViz

rotoViz.com is an awesome site that provides an innovative approach to projecting players from week-to-week: player comparables. Using their "GLSP (Game Level Similarity Projections) App," you can uncover "player comps" for any player in any given matchup. Here's how they explain the process:

> The idea behind GLSP is that we take the search for games against an opponent and make two changes to widen the search. We widen the search to include similar players and also similar defenses. So instead of just looking at DeMarco Murray against the Giants defense we would also look at Frank Gore's game against the Giants defense. Gore and Murray touch the ball a similar number of times per game and they are roughly the same size. But then we would also look at Murray's game against the Eagles defense. The Giants defense and Eagles defense allow roughly similar numbers to opposing RBs. All of this searching is done with a simple algorithm that scores each matchup by similarity. After 25 similar matchups have been found we can look at the fantasy scoring in those games in order to get some expectation of what might happen when Murray faces the Giants defense.

In my view, player comps offer two primary advantages when projecting players. First, they allow you to bypass the problem of a small sample size. Instead of looking at a handful of games in which a player faced a particular defense, you can look at a whole bunch of situations in which a comparable player was matched up against a similar D.

That allows for the second primary advantage: thinking of projections in terms of probabilities. When you see player projections, they are often "mean projections"—the average of what that player might do if he played the same opponent 1,000 times.

Sometimes the mean is useful. Other times, it's not. Two players might be projected for the exact same stat line, but one might be a far more volatile option than the other.

The GLSP App allows you to not only identify that volatility, but also quantify it. So now instead of projecting DeMarco Murray at something like 80 rushing yards, you can say "well, he has a 60 percent chance to rush for around 40 yards, but an abnormally high 40 percent probability of going off for about 190 yards."

The results aren't that black-and-white, but the point is that it can be incredibly useful to view projections in terms of probabilities. That helps to recognize player volatility, which is extremely vital in daily fantasy sports.

Subjectivity Through an Objective Framework

Due to the nature of the NFL, it's really difficult—perhaps impossible at the current moment—to create a totally objective model that can just spit out projections. There's still a heck of a lot of subjectivity in fantasy football—more so than in any other fantasy sport.

But I'm a big believer that the path to optimal subjective decision-making is paved with objectivity. By that, I mean that there's lots of value in sorting through the data, performing research and analyzing trends. Even if there's no completely objective way to implement that data, *the process itself is valuable.*

Through the combination of film study and analytics, you can more appropriately identify value plays versus overpriced commodities. By continually getting enough exposure to the values and fading the overpriced payers, you can become a long-term winner.

MLB-Specific Research

If the NFL were a teenager, MLB would be its nerdy, analytical little brother. Whereas football is very situation-dependent and rather disordered, baseball is more universal and far less chaotic. For the most part, we see the same sort of situations again and again on the diamond, and that allows us to place more weight on the MLB data we can collect.

As I mentioned, football can ironically become predictable *because* of the randomness inherent to the sport. When others are jumping on "hot" commodities or avoiding "injury prone" players, you can garner value by realizing that much of what we perceive in the NFL doesn't necessarily have a consistently repeatable cause.

Due to the lack of extreme randomness over a large sample size of baseball games, however, you can approach your research in a much different fashion—even the opposite—from football. While there's plenty of variance from night to night in MLB, those peaks and valleys even out over the long-run.

Whereas Aaron Rodgers faces even division opponents just twice a year, for example, Mike Trout can accumulate dozens and dozens of at-bats against individual pitchers. And if you want to take a broader approach and analyze Trout against, say, all lefties instead of a specific left-handed pitcher, there's a huge amount of reliable, standardized data.

Understanding Value in MLB

Before getting into some sites that can be of value to you if you plan to play daily fantasy baseball, I want to hit on how the differences in randomness should affect how you view value in each sport.

Regardless of everything else going on around you—streaks, matchups, advanced stats, news, whatever—your goal is always, always to find players who are underpriced, i.e. their projection exceeds their cost. There are different formulas to measure the amount of money you need to spend per point that will help you judge value—I'll detail those later—but that's always the goal.

Normally, the sorts of players who offer value in the NFL are those who are coming off of poor performances for reasons that aren't likely to remain consistent: poor matchups, unusual game situations, and so on.

On the other hand, MLB value (not necessarily player production, but value) is more independent of previous games. One major reason for that is because daily fantasy sites need to update MLB salaries every day, whereas NFL salaries get updated just once a week. In the latter sport, salaries often shift rapidly based on a very small sample of data. You want to capitalize on that artificial movement.

Baseball salaries, on the other hand, usually don't fluctuate as much. The sites don't overreact to individual performances because there are so many games, giving you a splendid (I don't know why I used the word 'splendid'? Literally never did that before, probably won't do it again) opportunity to generate value on players facing a poor pitcher, those playing in a "hitter's park," perhaps those in the midst of a hot streak, and so on.

Having said that, it's important to understand that you aren't *guaranteed* to find value on a football player who is coming off of a couple poor performances or a baseball player who is hitting the crap out of the ball. It's still all about a comparison of projection to salary.

FanGraphs

When it comes to MLB data and analysis, there's one site that sticks out above all others—FanGraphs.

FanGraphs is a Sabermetrics-lover's wet dream. The site displays all sorts of advanced stats that hold pragmatic value to daily fantasy owners: Weighted On-Base Average (wOBA), Weighted Runs Created (wRC), Home Runs per Fly Ball (HR/FB), Outside-the-Zone Swing Rate (O-Swing%), Fastball Runs Above Average (wFB), and so on.

Using the data, you can go as deep as to examine a lineup's ability to create runs over average on fastballs when facing a pitcher who has a below-average heater. It's just a little bit superior to the I-like-picking-players-from-my-home-team approach that you'll undoubtedly face quite a bit.

In addition, FanGraphs has made all of the data very accessible. There are detailed explanations for everything on the site. You can even create your own graphs for a variety of players in numerous advanced statistical categories, giving you the ability to quickly visualize the numbers in a way that many find helpful.

When combined with the comprehensive sites that I listed to start this chapter—RotoGrinders, Fantasy Pros, etc—FanGraphs is basically everything you need to get started in the world of daily fantasy baseball.

Daily Baseball Data

Whereas weather is important in daily fantasy football when assessing matchups, it's absolutely critical in fantasy baseball since games regularly get rained out. Depending on how you diversify your lineups, a rainout could potentially kill your profitability in a given day. It's essential to make sure there's very little chance of inclement weather when picking your players.

DailyBaseballData.com is the site many of daily fantasy's pros use for weather information. The site provides up-to-date information on the temperature, chance of precipitation, and wind speed for every game. Many pros actually start their daily fantasy baseball research at DailyBaseballData.com, checking the weather to immediately eliminate potential players.

That can be useful when you're choosing players in games that might not start within the next hour or two, but also note that DraftKings has a late player swap feature. That means that if the weather takes a turn after you've already submitted your lineup (and other games have begun) you can substitute in any players in games that have not yet started.

And now, lady (Hi Mom!) and gentlemen, it's time for the first piece of DraftKings data: the percentage of lineups using the late player swap feature.

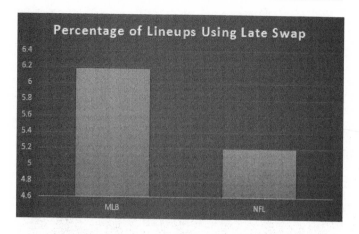

As you'd expect, more lineups use the late swap in MLB because there are more unexpected absences from lineups. Players take days off even when they aren't injured (especially catchers), so it's definitely something to monitor, particularly on weekends when you'll typically submit your lineup hours before many of the games begin. If the weather takes a dramatic shift in the afternoon, for example, you'll want to utilize the DraftKings player swap.

In addition to weather data, DailyBaseballData.com has all kinds of other stats: batter vs. pitcher splits for upcoming games, a lineup dashboard, and bullpen usage, among other stuff. Come for the weather, stay for Yasiel Puig's career slugging percentage against Michael Wacha.

The 10 Laws of Daily Fantasy Research

Your daily fantasy profitability will only be as good as your projections, and your projections will only be as good as your ability to research. When it comes down to it, all of the other aspects of quality daily fantasy play are secondary to finding the right numbers and implementing them correctly. That's all.

With that said, here are my "10 Laws of Daily Fantasy Research"—the 10 take-home points from this chapter.

Law No. 1: Stay focused on relevant data.

If you go into your daily fantasy research without a plan of attack, you'll never come out alive. No, really, there have been thousands of daily fantasy-related deaths of late. Just tragic.

But seriously, in the same manner that scientists form a hypothesis before conducting research or experiments, you need a focus as to what kind of data and analysis you're seeking and how you'll use it to influence your lineup decisions.

Law No. 2: Search for predictive stats.

There's all kinds of useless junk out there masquerading as intelligent sports analysis. Like all of ESPN. When I say you need to be focused on relevant stats, I mean data that is predictive. If it can't help you make accurate predictions, it's not of any use to you.

In 2012, the Kansas City Chiefs recovered six fumbles. Guess what? No one gives a crap. Recovering a fumble is about as random as you can get in sports. There's a small correlation between *forced fumbles* from one year to the next, but trying to predict the team that ends up with the ball after it's on the ground is a total crapshoot. Thus, the fumble recovery stat is useless without knowledge of how many fumbles the Chiefs actually forced.

The point is that you can get lost in a maze of sports trivia if you aren't focused on searching for the right kind of stats, i.e. those that aid in forecasting.

Law No. 3: Use Vegas not just as a secondary resource, but as a foundation of your research.

Throughout middle school, there was a kid named Jonathan Brooks who used to copy all of my schoolwork—tests, homework, whatever. It was kind of annoying at first, but I let him do it because ~~I eventually didn't mind it~~ I'm a pussy.

JB wasn't the funniest clown in the circus, so for him, the reward far outweighed the risk with relatively lax cheating penalties. I doubt he performed a risk analysis prior to looking over my shoulder, but I respected his hustle.

Fast-forward 15 years and now I'm the one who's cheating. I copy the answers from the smart kid in the daily fantasy class—Vegas—and you should too.

The guys in Vegas can offer so much valuable information, whether in the form of game totals or player props, that it would be asinine to ignore their work. Regardless of the sport you play, the Vegas lines should be an essential part of your daily fantasy research.

Law No. 4: Harness the power of the experts.

Known as the "wisdom of the crowd," the aggregate of expert opinions is superior to almost all of the individual opinions taken in isolation. Sites like FantasyPros.com bring you aggregate projections and rankings for various sports, and the result has enormous practical value.

In terms of selecting players, you need to be more confident in guys on whom "the crowd" is down if you want to use them. It's not that you can't ever go against the grain—you should, in certain situations—but rather that when accounting for your own fallibility, it's difficult to be overly bullish on a player many well-respected experts are fading.

Law No. 5: Get on Twitter.

And not just to follow Amanda Bynes.

Law No. 6: Know the level of randomness inherent to each sport.

One of the fundamental aspects that should affect how you approach daily fantasy is how much trust you can put in the numbers, and that's largely controlled by the randomness involved with each sport.

In the NFL, you can use randomness to your advantage, targeting underachieving studs who are the victims of small samples. In MLB, you should typically use a different tactic, fading players who are down in favor of those riding a hot streak.

Law No. 7: Increase your relevant sample size whenever possible.

Some daily fantasy baseball players prefer to examine batter vs. pitcher stats in great detail, but many of the game's greats don't place much stock in those splits because they're typically a relatively small sample. Instead, many pros prefer simple lefty/righty splits because the sample is always large.

The problem of a small sample is the impetus behind the GLSP App at rotoViz. By broadening the data set to include player and defense "comps," you can actually enhance the accuracy of your NFL projections.

There are times when a small sample can be so extreme that is holds value, but as women will tell you, larger is usually better.

Law No. 8: Don't rely solely on the data.

Because of the nature of the sport, I truly believe you could become a profitable daily fantasy baseball player without ever watching a single MLB game. The data is just that important.

But that doesn't mean it's the best way to approach daily fantasy. The numbers are important—critical, even—but sometimes, it's okay to choose players in a way that doesn't completely fit the data. The best daily fantasy players are flexible, understanding that a rigid, unchanging player selection strategy is never optimal.

Law No. 9: But let data inform your "hunches."

The chief reason I find it acceptable to (at times) side with hunches over data is because, as you become a more experienced daily fantasy player, your gut feelings will be influenced by the data anyway. Performing daily fantasy research isn't just a means to an end; it is valuable in and of itself.

Law No. 10: Never think that your research is complete.

There should never come a point in time when you say "Okay, my lineups are set, I don't need to do any other research." Your daily fantasy decisions should be influenced by the process just as much as the end result.

Since the process of researching players, reading analysis, and collecting data is so important, it follows that it should extend indefinitely. At a certain point, you need to get off of Twitter and fill out some lineups, of course. But the idea that you're ever "finished" ignores the worth of the process.

"Success is a journey, not a destination. The doing is often more important than the outcome."

-    *Arthur Ashe*

2 Twenty Thousand Leagues Under the Sea: How to Pick Your leagues

"The quality of decision is like the well-timed swoop of a falcon which enables it to strike and destroy its victim."

- *Sun Tzu*

Do you know what that Sun Tzu quote has to do with daily fantasy sports? Not much, but I'm a big fan of Eastern Philosophy, so now it's in my book. Deal with it.

If we're going to draw some sort of meaning from the quote, though, let's go with this: every single decision you make as a daily fantasy player should have a purpose behind it. It should be a reflection of your goals.

There are all sorts of leagues types in daily fantasy, all of which require a different strategy from the others, sometimes drastically so. Further, there's not necessarily an objectively "best" league out there, just the best for you.

If you're a high-floor player looking to grind out profits, you should use head-to-head leagues and 50/50s as the foundation of your league selection. If you're a high-variance player seeking a big payday, GPPs—guaranteed prize pools— are your best bet.

For the uninitiated, I'm going to walk you through the various league types in this chapter. I'll provide some brief commentary and strategy suggestions, but the majority of the "well how can I freakin' win in these leagues?" material will be in subsequent sections.

Here, I'll lay out a plan of attack when selecting leagues, showing you how to increase your upside without taking on a significant amount of risk. I'll use DraftKings' leagues as the template since 1) they have every popular league type in the industry and 2) uh, yeah, hi, they've given me all kinds of data.

Let's go.

The Main Players

There are a few basic ways in which daily fantasy leagues differentiate themselves from one another: timing, commission, size, and payout structure.

Timing

By 'timing,' I mean when the league starts and ends, i.e. which professional games does it encapsulate? There aren't many different league times in MLB because they're typically true daily contests, whereas most NFL contests span a period over 24 hours.

In the NFL, you can play in leagues that start anywhere from the Thursday-night game all the way to "Primetime" leagues that don't kick off until the Sunday night game. Here's the basic idea that you need to know regarding league timing: the more players you need to analyze, the more likely it is that the better player will win.

Primetime leagues are fun because you can watch your entire lineup on national television, but they greatly enhance the amount of variance in the results, i.e. almost anyone can win (*almost*, since it's still a game of skill). That's not necessarily a bad thing; it's great for novice owners, actually.

If you believe you have an advantage over most other daily fantasy players, however, you want the player pool to be as large as possible, increasing the knowledge and skill needed to profit. That makes Thursday night and standard Sunday-Monday NFL games your best bet.

Thursday Night NFL

I'm giving Thursday NFL contests their own section because I think there's a ton of interesting aspects to these leagues. I've long discussed the value of Thursday NFL leagues, for two reasons.

First, people love to see their players on television, so they'll frequently add players from games that are on national TV, perhaps even if it's not the right move. When you join a Thursday night football GPP, for example, you'll run into dozens of lineups that are stacked with players from that night's game just because people want to watch their players. It's pretty ridiculous, actually.

Second, there's this...

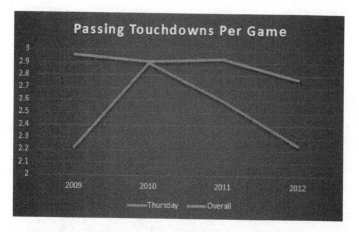

Overall, there's right around 10 percent less total fantasy production in Thursday night games as compared to all others. The NFL frequently rolls out some Thursday night matchups that make you seriously consider your girlfriend's request to watch Bravo. The teams are poor, yet that's not reflected in many lineups, so it seems like you could acquire a major advantage by shifting more of your NFL money to Thursday night leagues and then subsequently fading the players in that game.

BUT, thanks to DraftKings, we can now actually dig into the data to see what's going on in Thursday leagues versus those that start on Sunday. And this is really what daily fantasy is all about, too—testing theories in a scientific manner to see if what we "know" to be true is indeed the way we presume. So here's a look at some actual DraftKings data from the 2013 NFL season.

Although the effect seems small, keep in mind that these are the average scores over every single league. You can see there's a larger deviation in points in Thursday night leagues; the average lineup scores one less point than those in normal Sunday leagues, but the winning score is one point better.

To give you an idea of why those numbers are actually significant, consider a 5,000-team GPP in which the average score is 129. How many lineups would need to tank (we'll say that's a score of just 100, which would have no chance at winning anything) to get that average to drop to 128?

The answer is 174! It would take 174 lineups of just 100 points to drop the average from 129 to 128. That's 3.5 percent of lineups, which is very significant in a GPP.

What about if we consider lineups that are only slightly worse (say, 120 points)? It would actually take 555 of those lineups to drop the total average by one point! That's 11.1 percent! If you enter a GPP knowing 11.1 percent of lineups are going to score nine points lower than the average, that's quite the advantage, isn't it?

But what about the increase of one point for the average winning score? Three thoughts there. First, the winning scores naturally belong to those players who didn't submit sub-optimal lineups, so we'd never expect any sort of decline (for GPP winners, anyway) in Thursday night leagues.

Second, you might argue that players are more likely to combine a quarterback and one of his receivers in a Thursday night lineup since they want to see more of their guys play, which would naturally increase upside.

Third, and most important, there's an extra game to analyze for Thursday night leagues. In the same way that Primetime leagues have *lower* winning scores because there's a smaller pool of players, Thursday night leagues have *higher* winning scores because there's a larger sample of potentially valuable players to start. That one extra game might seem inconsequential, but it's enough to at least partially account for that one-point difference.

So, what's the final verdict on Thursday night NFL leagues? I think there's good evidence that there's some bad money in them. The average winning lineup is still high, but you should be able to match that jump with a larger pool of potential players. However, the decline in the average score—which takes place over a massive sample—suggests a decent percentage of Thursday lineups just don't have much of a chance.

Commission

In most low-entry leagues on DraftKings, the site pays back 90 percent of the total buy-ins. That means if you enter a head-to-head for $1, you'll get $1.80 if you win (your original $1 plus 80 cents). Enter for $5 and you'll win $9. The money that the daily fantasy sites keep when you play is known as the "commission."

Sportsbooks charge something similar, but here's the difference: you don't need to go up against a sportsbook when you play daily fantasy sports. You're going mano-a-mano with someone else just like you. Or worse.

So whereas there are probably only a handful of individuals in the world who can make a comfortable living betting sports long-term, the potential for profitability in daily fantasy is vastly superior. It's far easier to overcome that commission when you're facing my grandfather (loves DraftKings, loses all his money) instead of a sophisticated computer.

Size + Payout Structure

Daily fantasy leagues can vary from two players to into five figures (that's at least 10,000, Uncle Bruce). You should obviously approach those two extremes in very different manners. Two-man leagues—head-to-heads—are the safest leagues in most situations.

Typically, the greater the number of players in a league, the lower your win expectation. And that win expectation—the percentage of leagues you can realistically expect to win at each level—is crucial to your money management. If you're entering leagues as if you have a 50 percent win expectation when it's really closer to 25 percent, there's a solid chance your kids aren't getting presents this year.

However, the size of daily fantasy leagues can be misleading, so here's the most important piece of advice I can offer you when examining different leagues: look at the payout structure.

Let me start a new paragraph and write that again: look at the payout structure.

The size of the league can be important in understanding your upside and risk, but what matters most is 1) how often you'll cash and 2) how those funds are distributed among the winners.

Let's look at an example of how league size can be misleading. You enter two 100-man leagues with the same lineup. Your players perform slightly above-average, and you score in the 35th percentile in both leagues. In one you double your money, and in another you lose your entry fee. What's the deal?

One of those leagues was a 50/50—a league in which the top half of entrants get paid and the bottom half lose their money. The other was a 100-man GPP in which only the top 15 entrants cashed.

Knowing those payout structures, should you really have submitted the same lineup to both leagues? Probably not. In the 50/50, you took on minimal risk since half of the 100 players cashed. If you're a completely average player, you'd finish right around the 50th percentile, on average, over the long-run.

Your risk was much greater in the 100-man GPP, however, with fewer than one-in-six entrants cashing. Even the world's top daily fantasy players probably couldn't cash more than, say, 30 percent of the time in such leagues, meaning their expectation is always "I'm probably going to lose my entry fee in this league." The upside can of course negate that risk, but it's crucial that you understand how the risk affects your approach.

In my first daily fantasy book, I analyzed how the payout structure affects your ability to cash:

> *Let's look at the minimum winning percentage you must maintain to break even over the long-run. The first number after each league type is the winning percentage needed in a league that pays out 90 percent of entry fees, the second number assumes eight percent commission (92 percent payouts), and the third number is the winning percentage in a truly random league.*

> - *Head-to-Head or 50/50: 55.5 percent/54.3 percent/50.0 percent*
> - *3-Team League (Pays out one): 37.0 percent/36.2 percent/33.3 percent*

- **5-Team League (Pays out one): 22.2 percent/21.7 percent/20.0 percent**

For the record, the formula to determine breakeven percentage is as follows:

- **B = N*(F/P), where B is breakeven percentage, N is number of people paid, F is fee to play, and P is total payout**

In a hypothetical 10-team league that pays out just one person and charges 10 percent to play, the formula would be Breakeven = 1*(50/450) = .1111 = 11.11 percent.

You don't necessarily need to incorporate the breakeven percentages in every aspect of your daily fantasy prep, but make sure you understand how the payout structure of leagues affects how much money you sink into them.

As a quick aside, I want to touch on a few other league types you'll run into on DraftKings.

Multipliers

Multipliers are leagues in which you can instantly triple, quadruple, quintuple, or 10-ruple (what?) your money. They range from moderately risky (triple-ups) to extremely risky (10x boosters). The amount of money you put into each multiplier and the strategy you employ when selecting your lineup should depend on the payout structure and your anticipated win percentage.

Qualifiers

Qualifiers are leagues in which the prize pool consists of qualifying tickets to larger tournaments. Qualifiers are really unique in that you can't necessarily approach them like other leagues since they're actually very high-risk with huge upside.

Let's say you enter an $11 qualifier with 100 people, for example, in which the top 10 win a $100 qualifying ticket to a larger tournament. If you finish in the top 10, you can enter another 100-man tournament for free with that ticket, and if you're a pro, maybe it has a $130 expected value or so for you. That's awesome.

But if that subsequent tournament also cashes just the top 10 entrants, chances are the ticket won't return anything for you. That highlights the difference between expected value and money in the bank. Over an infinite sample size and with an infinite bankroll, you'd cash enough that qualifiers wouldn't be any riskier than a head-to-head leagues.

Unfortunately, you don't have unlimited funds for no reason whatsoever (I'm looking at you Mr. Flacco), so it's not like you can put 10 percent of your bankroll into each qualifier hoping to win. While one-in-10 entrants received qualifying tickets, most of those tickets ended up being fruitless. Instead of a 10 percent win expectation for an average player, the actual expectation is just one percent (a one-in-10 chance multiplied by a one-in-10 chance). That could really affect your strategy, huh?

That doesn't mean qualifiers are poor investments, however. First, they're absolutely fine if you're treating them for what they are—leagues in which there's often high risk but also enormous upside. Second, there's typically a lot of "bad money" in qualifiers; if your bankroll is high enough to support them, qualifiers offer an outstanding long-term money-making opportunity. Third, many qualifiers often have overlay.

Overlay

If you don't know what overlay is, it's about to become your new favorite word. Just typing it puts a smile on my face. O-ver-lay. So beautiful.

Overlay is a situation in which the total amount of entry money in a league is less than what the site must pay out. It occurs in GPPs and it's a daily fantasy player's best friend.

If you enter a 100-man league with a guaranteed payout at a $10 entry point, the site will pay out in the neighborhood $900, no matter what. So you're putting down $10 to win $9.

But sometimes the leagues don't fill. Actually, it happens all across the daily fantasy industry because the sites are still very much in the customer-acquisition stage of development (and will be for a while), so they basically pay you to play. It's a mutually beneficial relationship.

When the leagues don't fill and the site loses money, bada bing bada boom, you have overlay. In that hypothetical 100-man league, 90 entrants is the breakeven point for the site. If the league has fewer than 90 players, the site will lose money. Sucks for them, awesome for us.

The greater the overlay, the crappier you can be to still make money. If you're an average player in the aforementioned 100-man league that fills just 90—meaning the site breaks even—your expectation is just the entry fee ($10).

If only 75 people enter the league, however, you can be an average player and still be in a positive expected value situation. Since there would be a total of $750 in the pot but the site must unload $900, your expectation on a $10 investment as a totally average player would be $12. If you could play an infinite number of such leagues, you'd see a guaranteed 20 percent return.

Overlay is kind of like beer: it turns an average girl into a pretty one and a pretty one into a supermodel. Even if you're just an average girl at the bar, consistently exposing yourself to overlay can make your bankroll look way more attractive.

Multi-Entry

Multi-entry leagues are those in which you can. . .you guessed it. . .enter multiple times (no way!). Multi-entry leagues are really unique because they can be used as a hedge against excessive risk.

Imagine you have $100 to spend in GPPs. You could enter a single tournament at that buy-in level, but chances are you'd lose your Benjamin. But if you split up that $100 into 10 different lineups in a single multi-entry, you could greatly enhance the probability of cashing.

That's made possible since you can diversify your lineups in a way that increases your floor and reduces your ceiling. The risk of a single GPP entry at $100 is losing everything, and that would probably happen at least 75 percent of the time, assuming you're an average player (and that's the best-case scenario on a site like DraftKings that pays out a really high percentage of entrants).

The probability of losing all of your money with 10 lineups in a multi-entry is far less, though. In a league that pays out the top quarter of entrants, the odds of losing on all 10 lineups would be just 5.6 percent for the average player.

More entries isn't always better, though. Imagine you could enter every single lineup into a 100-man GPP. You'd win the entire payout, but you'd lose whatever the site charged you in commission, assuming the league filled up and there was no overlay.

Further, at a certain point, you don't want to keep diversifying your lineups. Your goal is to maximize your expected return, not do everything possible to increase your probability of cashing. At a certain point, diversifying lineups becomes detrimental because you'll start to use sub-optimal players, which obviously limits your financial upside.

There's no single formula that can tell you the "correct" number of lineups to use in a multi-entry league because it's a fluid situation, dependent on your projections and values from day to day and week to week.

But here's a simple rule-of-thumb: unless you think you're a well below-average player, the expected value of multi-entry lineups in a league with overlay is positive, i.e. go nuts.

Diversifying Your League Portfolio

I conversed with a bunch of daily fantasy's top players prior to writing this book, all of whom had different strategies from one another when it comes to selecting leagues. Mike5754, for example, plays very few tournaments and grinds out profits via almost exclusively head-to-head and 50/50 leagues, while naapstermaan plays almost exclusively in tournaments.

The manner in which you diversify your leagues is a fluid situation, but most players find themselves somewhere near the center of the spectrum, playing a combination of head-to-heads, tournaments, and other league types. It's really a "favorite flavor" sort of situation

Your particular league structure should be a reflection of your willingness to assume risk. If you have a $500 bankroll and you care more about turning that into $50,000 than $1,000, you'll probably be better off playing single-lineup 50/50s and tournaments in order to increase your ceiling and quickly grow your bankroll. If you want to grind out profits, you should find yourself closer to the risk-averse end of the spectrum.

Playing It Safe

Another aspect of league selection you need to consider is how it affects the amount of cash you can have in play in a given day. If you're playing exclusively tournaments, for example, you could be in big trouble if you're putting even 10 percent of your bankroll into play, depending how you diversify your lineups.

On the other hand, you can justify using 10 percent of your bankroll at one time if you're entering primarily head-to-head leagues. Some pros put even more of their bankroll into play at any given time, hedging through safe league selection and lineup diversification.

No matter what types of leagues you play and lineups you use, though, you can't put all of your money into play in a single day. Even if you think there's only a 0.5 percent chance of that "oh shit I just finished in the bottom one percent of lineups" sort of day, it will eventually strike you if you play long enough.

The best players put themselves in a position to capitalize off of variance, not get destroyed by it.

The 10 Laws of Daily Fantasy League Selection

Your league selection and diversification is vital in reaching your goals. Here are the 10 most crucial points from Chapter 2.

Law No. 1: Know that the greater the player pool, the more skill required to win.

The more players you need to analyze, the higher the probability of the best man winning. That's beneficial for experienced players, but not for newbies. Novices might want to consider leagues with smaller pools, such as Primetime NFL leagues or MLB leagues on days during which only a few MLB teams are playing.

Law No. 2: Understand the game theory involved with Thursday night leagues.

I was chatting with my brother the other day and he mentioned that he's going to stop entering so many Thursday night leagues because the games are always so low-scoring. I got unnecessarily angry at that assessment because, hey, if you don't take fantasy sports so seriously that it ruins relationships, you just aren't doing it right.

Anyway, I got mad because the low-scoring nature of Thursday night games—about 10 percent less overall fantasy production—is one of the primary reasons they hold so much value. No one said you need to select players in the actual Thursday night game, yet so many daily fantasy players do just that.

Because you know that lineups will be generally sub-optimal because people want to watch their guys on national television, you can enter lots of Thursday leagues. Better yet, you can fade the Thursday night players because of 1) their expected lack of production and 2) their abundance in others' lineups to instantly gain an advantage right out of the gate.

Law No. 3: Recognize the risks and upside involved with Thursday night leagues.

On most daily fantasy sites, your lineups lock after the Thursday night league (or any contest type) begins. Not so on DraftKings. Like I said, you can remove and add any players who are in games that haven't yet started.

That's important because it allows you to enter a truly optimal lineups. For example, you can use a quarterback listed as "Questionable" in a Thursday night league or a pitcher starting in a night game that could rain out. On other sites, that would be needlessly risky because, if your quarterback or pitcher don't play, you get a zero in those spots.

On DraftKings, you can just substitute in anyone who hasn't yet played. That reduces the risk involved with the early player selection of Thursday night leagues or weekend MLB games, yet you still hold onto the upside of playing in a league with 1) a larger pool of players and 2) a bunch of novices starting players who they want to see play on national TV.

Law No. 4: Prior to joining a league, first check the payout structure.

The number of people in a league is far less important than the payout structure. You could have 100,000 people in a 50/50, and you're still getting paid if you're in the top half. The range and deviation of the payout structure, not the size of the league, should dictate your actions.

Note that before writing this book, I had basically chosen DraftKings as my "home" daily fantasy site. There are a few reasons for that, but one is their tournament payout structure. In most GPPs, the top quarter (or at least top 20 percent) of entrants cash, and that greatly reduces the risk involved with placing a relatively large portion of your cash into tournaments.

Law No. 5: Second, calculate the commission.

The commission is the percentage of money the daily sites "charge" to play. It's simple to calculate: just divide the money they pay out into the total money in the league. So a $50 heads-up match that pays $90 to the winner has a 10 percent commission. All other things equal, you want to enter leagues with as little commission as possible.

Law No. 6: Always seek overlay.

Overlay is like "anti-commission." It's when a GPP doesn't fill and the site will lose money in a league, thus "paying you" to play. Always, always, always try to put yourself into as many overlay situations as possible.

In a league with overlay, an average player is +EV. Whereas an average player would see somewhere around a -10 percent ROI over the long run in a standard league with a 10 percent commission, he'd make money if he entered nothing but GPPs with overlay.

Law No. 7: Don't enter qualifiers as if you're winning "real" money.

If you're calculating the amount of money you can put into qualifiers as if you can "cash out" after the qualifier has ended, you're going to spend too much.

Here's a good metaphor for daily fantasy qualifiers. Someone offers you 10:1 odds on rolling any single number on a fair die. You decide to put a certain percentage of your cash down on your roll, but then he proclaims that you absolutely *must* roll three straight times—three separate bets—and win all three rolls to cash.

That little tidbit should dramatically alter the way you approach this scenario. Instead of having a one-in-six chance of rolling the coveted number, it's just one-in-216 if you have to get it correct three consecutive times. The stipulation of the agreement significantly changes the odds.

That's kind of what qualifiers do. Although the potential return is ultimately still there, it takes a long time to see it; qualifiers extend the number of "rolls" to which you need to commit.

Law No. 8: Enter multiple lineups into leagues until 1) it compromises your bankroll or 2) the lineups no longer possess a positive expected return.

Multi-entry leagues can provide the opportunity to hedge against a poor night or week because you can diversify your lineups as much as you'd like. That's particularly useful in baseball—a sport in which you can roll out multiple lineup combos to "cover your bases," so to speak. See what I did there? Puns. So hot right now.

Entering multiple lineups into a single tournament is beneficial to a point. First, you obviously never want to compromise the integrity of your bankroll. Second, you should always start with your optimal lineup, so each subsequent lineup will be a little be worse than the one before it. Once you can no longer expect a positive return on your investment, it's time to step away from the computer, dude.

Law No. 9: Don't put too much money in play if you enter primarily tournaments.

This is fairly obvious, but if you know for a fact that you'll likely lose a league that you enter (which is pretty much the case with anything other than head-to-heads or 50/50s), you shouldn't be putting too much money down on it.

DraftKings allows for a totally different tournament strategy because their payouts kick ass, but many sites pay out, like, less than five percent of entrants in some tourneys, which sucks.

So if you're entering such a risky league type, you really can't even put down one percent of your total bankroll. You'd win once in every 20 entries as an average player, but it's not inconceivable that you could play 100 straight leagues without cashing once.

And if that league costs, say, $10, you'd need at least a $1,000 bankroll to even consider entering it. I have way more than that because I'm a baller, but lots of people don't. If you're entering high-risk tournaments with buy-ins that are too high, you'll go broke. If you were to place five percent of your bankroll ($10 of a $200 bankroll, for example) into a league that cashes out the top five percent, you'd have just a 50 percent chance—a coin flip!—to cash before losing all of your money.

Law No. 10: Make every league decision based upon your willingness to assume risk.

If you have a small bankroll and don't mind taking some big risks for the opportunity at a huge cash, then you can play a whole lot differently than if you're trying to grind out a two percent return each week. Know your goals and use them to determine the proper league selection for you.

"The essence of strategy is that you must set limits on what you're trying to accomplish."

- *Michael Porter*

3 One-on-One: How to Win Heads-Up Leagues (and 50/50s)

"Success is steady progress toward one's personal goals."

- *Jim Rohn*

You know what I like to discuss with my friends who play daily fantasy? Tournaments. GPPs. Large-field leagues. Whatever you want to call it, we like to talk about how awesome it would be to win DraftKings' Millionaire Grand Final.

You know what most pros like to discuss? Head-to-heads and 50/50s. With the exception of naapstermaan—the king of tournaments—and a few other players, many of daily fantasy's top players build their bankroll by kicking ass in head-to-heads, 50/50s, and the like. They take advantage of tournaments, too, but they utilize smaller leagues for steadier growth.

Head-to-heads and other small leagues that pay out a high percentage of entrants are foundational pieces of the daily fantasy pie. The upside isn't as great as in a tournament, but neither is the risk. And if you're really trying to see a quality ROI in daily fantasy, you need to minimize risk in some form or another.

There are two primary ways in which head-to-head leagues in particular minimize risk. First, the obvious: there are only two freakin' players. Even if you're new to daily fantasy, you'll still probably win at least 40 percent of your heads-up matches.

Second, head-to-head leagues allow for a linear return. By that, I mean that if you consistently finish in the top 25 percent of all scores, you'll get paid at that rate (winning in three-quarters of your heads-up leagues). If you're a totally average player near the 50th percentile, you'll probably win right around as many as you lose.

That's in opposition to tournaments in which you need to cross a certain tipping point to get paid. A 50th percentile score isn't going to do you any good; it will never win.

50/50s

Like a heads-up league, the top half of entrants in a 50/50 get paid. That can create safety if you're entering just one lineup. No matter the quality of your lineup in a heads-up match, there's always a chance that it gets beat by a higher score. That won't happen in a 50/50, however, since you won't see an outlier take you down.

However, here's why head-to-head games are safer when we look at the broad picture: the more you play, the less risky they become. With head-to-heads, you can enter the same lineup again and again and actually *increase* the safety of that lineup; the larger the sample size, the more likely that you'll get paid "as you should," i.e. there will be a linear relationship between your score and your return.

If you have a top 10 percent score, for example, and enter it into just one league, you'll have a 90 percent chance to win.

Enter it into 10 leagues, and the odds of not getting paid are basically zero. Enter it into 1,000 leagues, and you'll be nearly guaranteed to win close to 90 percent and lose close to 10 percent.

Now consider a single lineup in 50/50s. One 50/50? Lots of safety? Two 50/50s. A little less safety. Five-hundred 50/50s? You better be on your game, bro. Because if that team flops and you entered it into nothing but 50/50s, you just lost all of your money.

Heads-up leagues are like schools of fish: they have safety in numbers. Meanwhile, 50/50s are similar to pancakes. As Mitch Hedberg would have said, they're all exciting at first, but after a while you're fu**ing sick of 'em.

Diversifying Based on Player Pool

Theoretically, 50/50s would be invaluable if you were playing completely different lineups. You could enter various lineups into different 50/50s and just use those to grow your bankroll.

The problem with that strategy is that, as you move down your list of lineups, they become less and less optimized. The value of submitting one lineup into lots of leagues is that you can play the best of the best. Over the long-run, that will provide you with the best return.

So it's really a balancing act between diversifying lineups and increasing upside. That means your potential player pool— the number of players you like in a given night in MLB or a given weekend in the NFL—should dictate your strategy.

Namely, if you like relatively few players, you'll have fewer lineups and would be smart to play in more head-to-head matchups. Meanwhile, a larger player pool would allow for greater lineup diversity, and thus more opportunity to enter 50/50s.

Raise the ~~Roof~~ Floor

One of the most overrated stats in all of football is yards per carry (YPC). The stat is pretty much useless because it's so affected by outliers. A running back can be having a poor game of 15 carries for 45 yards (3.0 YPC), then break off a 70-yard run that will catapult his average to 7.19 YPC. All of a sudden, he "ran all over the defense"—a conclusion that might result from one broken tackle or a defender falling down.

Is that 115 yards on 16 carries really the same as a running back who continually gashes the defense for seven yards? Of course not, and it's vital to understand that difference when selecting your fantasy lineups.

In his book *Antifragile*, Nassim Nicholas Taleb makes a distinction between the resilient and the antifragile. The resilient can withstand shock; it remains the same in the face of outliers. The antifragile, on the other hand, not only withstands variance, but it prospers from it. The antifragile *improves* with chaos.

In many ways, your daily fantasy lineup selection should be built upon a similar foundation. Outlying poor performances will hurt you regardless of the league type, obviously, but you want your head-to-head lineups to be as resilient as possible; you want consistent play from every position. When a 40th percentile lineup is a winner in 50/50s and most head-to-heads, you want low-variance, not volatility.

Understanding Long-Term Trends

In any daily fantasy sport, you have a lot of decisions on your hands, the most overlooked of which might be salary cap allocation. The individual matchups are of course important and every lineup should be built upon specific information relative to that day's games, but I think some players overlook the importance of long-term trends.

While the value of an individual player is fleeting, the importance and consistency of specific positions is more everlasting. Are quarterbacks generally safer options than running backs? Is it ever okay to pay up for a kicker? Which types of wide receivers provide consistent production?

NFL Head-to-Head and 50/50 Strategy

Head-to-head or 50/50, what you're seeking is consistency. If you average 150 points with half of your lineups scoring 100 points and the other half scoring 200 points, you're actually not going to be a profitable heads-up player. If you can find a way to score around 150 points each time, however, you'll be nearly unbeatable over the long-run.

To back up that idea, let's take a look at some more DraftKings data, this time on the average scores in different league types. Of all the charts you'll see in this book, this one will probably end up being the most popular because of all the information it contains.

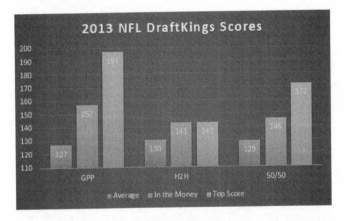

This is awesome stuff. I'm going to get into more detail on the GPP section in the next chapter, but you can see the average top score (197) and average score that finishes in the money (157) dwarf the numbers in head-to-heads and 50/50s.

Looking at those head-to-head and 50/50 leagues, the average top score in the latter is much higher than that in the former, which is to be expected since there are just more lineups (sometimes many more so) in 50/50s. Nothing strange there.

But here's what's most interesting to me. The average "in the money" score in head-to-heads (143) is three points lower than that in 50/50s (146). Since the top half of entrants get paid in both league types and we're dealing with a huge sample size, you'd expect the numbers to be equal. You'll have more outliers in a 50/50 since there are more lineups, but if you took the same sample of heads-up lineups, you'd think that the score distribution and average would be the same.

But it's not. Further, despite a higher average "in the money" score in 50/50s, the average overall score is one point *lower* than in head-to-head leagues. That means the deviation between the average score and the average winning score in 50/50s (17 points) is a lot higher than the same deviation in heads-up matches (only 13 points).

Here's my explanation for the difference that, if true, could really alter the way you enter both league types: *people are approaching 50/50 leagues with the wrong strategy*. It initially seems like 50/50s might be more difficult since the average "in the money" score is three points higher than in heads-up matches, but I don't think that's the case.

Instead, I think many daily fantasy players are approaching 50/50s with a high-variance strategy much like what you might seek in a GPP. So there's a wide gap between the best scores and the average scores that increases the overall average, but *the outlying top lineups might be throwing off the mean.*

Here's a visualization. First, this is how scores might be distributed in a 10-man 50/50 league in which players submit optimal lineups.

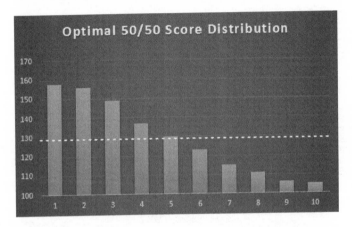

This sample distribution matches the DraftKings data—an average "in the money" score of 146 and an average overall score of 129. The dotted line represents that average. You can see that half of the 10 lineups finish above that 129 mean, which is what we'd expect if players submit lineups as they should with a low-variance strategy in mind.

However, this is an example of what we actually see with 50/50 lineups.

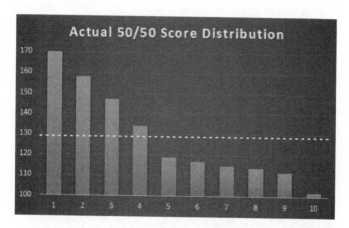

Again, the average of the "in the money" scores is still 146 and the overall mean is still 129. But there's a larger deviation in scores, so the top lineups make it seem as though players are better when they're really just submitting high-risk/high-reward lineups.

Now, here's the important part. Take a look at the average lineup dotted line. It's still at 129, but now there are only four lineups that fall above it. The fifth-best lineup—one that would cash in this 50/50 league—has just 119 points, which is 10 below the overall average.

So despite the higher average score in 50/50s over head-to-heads, the deviation in points suggests *you might be able to cash in them more easily.* Daily fantasy players might see the large number of entrants in a 50/50 (which can be huge at times) and automatically think they need a high-variance lineup with lots of upside. That creates a phenomenon through which below-average lineups can sneak into the money.

In reality, you should approach a 50/50 just like a head-to-head league. In both, you want a high floor. There are three primary areas on which to focus in order to increase it as much as possible: position consistency, player types, and player combinations.

NFL Position Consistency

For the most part, daily fantasy players don't pay much for kickers. Amateurs and pros alike understand that it's usually senseless to pay top-dollar for a position that's not consistent from week to week. It doesn't matter how many points a player scores and it doesn't matter how scarce those points are if you can't predict his performance.

We all seem to intuitively know that we shouldn't pay for kickers, but few people extend this argument to the other positions. In leagues in which safety is the name of the game, there should be a strong positive correlation between the percentage of cap space you're willing to spend on a player and your ability to accurately project his performance.

It's not like any of the skill positions are unpredictable in the same way as kickers, but there's still varying degrees of predictability. Those should undoubtedly have an influence on your decision-making. All other things equal, you could maximize your team's long-term floor by allocating a higher percentage of the cap to the safest players.

In my first book on daily fantasy, I calculated the consistency of each position. I'm going to use the same methodology here, but with updated results. To obtain the numbers, I looked at the top fantasy scorers over the past four years. They are the players who would typically cost the most money on daily fantasy sites.

I charted the number of "startable" weeks for the players at each position. A "startable" week was defined as finishing in the top 33 percent at the position (among the top 30 quarterbacks, tight ends, defenses, and kickers and the top 75 running backs and wide receivers).

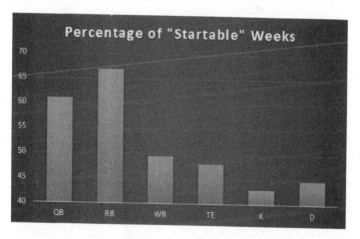

You can see that running backs have been by far the most consistent position, with the best of the bunch giving you a top 10 performance 67.0 percent of the time. Quarterbacks aren't far behind at 61.1 percent, but no other position is close.

When you think about it, that shouldn't be a surprise. Consider the number of opportunities each position has per game. For quarterbacks, it might be 35 attempts. For top running backs, it's in the range of 15 to 25 touches.

Meanwhile, wide receivers and tight ends might be lucky to see 10 targets in a game, and it's often much fewer. Just based on those numbers alone, you'd expect quarterbacks and running backs to be more consistent, and thus more predictable. It's like asking if a baseball player will come closer to hitting at his career average after five games or after 20 games. . .there's just no contest.

Taking it a step further, I analyzed the percentage of "top-tier" weeks turned in by each position. I defined "top-tier" as a top two finish for quarterbacks, tight ends, kickers, and defenses or a top five finish for running backs and wide receivers (the top 6.7 percent for each position).

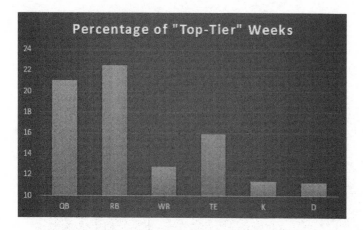

Again, no contest. Quarterbacks and running backs are just far more consistent on a week-to-week basis than all other positions. When you're paying for reliability, you should start with the quarterback and running back positions.

NFL Player Types

The position consistency data is certainly useful in all league types, but we can cut up the data a little more to obtain even better accuracy. Specifically, we can look at subsections of each position to see which *types* of players are the most consistent, and thus worthy of the majority of our cap space in head-to-head leagues.

Before diving into that, I think it's important to once again rehash the fact that much of what we view as individual consistency and volatility in the NFL is illusory. Would we ever create enduring narratives for baseball players through eight games? Never, so why do it for NFL players?

I explained this idea in *Fantasy Football for Smart People: How to Cash in on the Future of the Game*:

> In any set of random (or near-random) data, you'll see lots of "abnormal" results. If you assign Calvin Johnson a 50 percent chance of going for 100 yards and a touchdown in any given game, he'll probably wind up with somewhere around eight games with such numbers over the course of a season.

> But there's also a solid chance that he'll appear to have either an unusually outstanding or a very poor year. With a 50 percent chance of 100 yards and a score in any game, Megatron is around as likely to have either five or 12 stellar games as he is to have exactly eight.

> Because the number of games in an NFL season is so low, it's really easy to see patterns in data that aren't really there. Over the course of even a few NFL seasons, we'd expect some players to appear to have a huge degree of weekly consistency, even if consistency were completely random.

> Similarly, even with total randomness, a handful of players would appear to be "all-or-nothing" fantasy options without much consistency, when in reality

> *they possess just as much consistency as the most reliable performers.*

I really believe daily fantasy players as a whole place too much stock in past game-to-game consistency on the individual level, especially in the NFL. It's not that game-to-game consistency doesn't exist, but just that it's going to be really, really difficult for us to separate it from randomness.

It's the same reasoning behind my typically bullish stance on injury-prone players. Are some players more likely to get injured than others? Probably, but that doesn't mean we can turn that idea into actionable information.

Injuries are relatively low-frequency events controlled heavily by randomness, and humans aren't built to properly deal with randomness. We perceive all sorts of signals that aren't really there because it's not all that evolutionarily beneficial to say "I don't know."

But in daily fantasy sports, saying "I don't know" is a great thing; by factoring your own fallibility into your decisions—a choice that's reflected in your stance on week-to-week consistency and injury-proneness alike—you'll be able to acquire value where others are overlooking it.

The bottom line is that the majority of what most think they see as consistent play is noise. It would take years of NFL data to establish individual player consistency to the point that we can trust what we're seeing isn't just randomness. By that time, it's too late.

The crux of my individual-player-consistency-is-kind-of-overhyped-but-maybe-not-completely argument is that a small sample size hinders our ability to obtain meaningful results.

The solution? Once again, it's player comps. By broadening the potential player pool to include players who resemble the one in question, we can actually acquire more significant results. Ultimately, it just comes down to figuring out which sorts of players—and which aspects of their games—are consistent and repeatable.

Quarterbacks

Many NFL teams covet versatility, particularly on the offensive side of the ball, because it can create matchup problems. As a daily fantasy football player, your search for versatility should be more league-specific.

Namely, versatility is a wonderful thing in head-to-head matchups or leagues with a high percentage of players cashing (50/50s and even three-team leagues, too). Versatility increases the number of ways a player can beat a defense, raising his floor.

At the quarterback position, mobile quarterbacks like Cam Newton and Michael Vick have proven to be more consistent than the average passer. That flies in the face of conventional wisdom, which suggests that quarterbacks who rely on their legs are actually big risks.

I looked at the number of quality starts from mobile passers—those who have rushed for over 400 yards in a season—with "quality start" being defined as any game in which the quarterback posted at least six percent of his total fantasy points. That way, I could automatically adjust for differences in total production to see which passers have a flatter distribution of scores, i.e. more consistency.

It turns out that the mobile passers have been just under 10 percent more consistent than pocket passers. The idea that a player like Newton is volatile, which probably stems from the perception that he might not be an elite passer, is just wrong.

Running Backs

As I mentioned earlier, I was very bearish on Marshawn Lynch heading into the 2013 season. I ended up looking like an idiot, but part of my reasoning was that Lynch was becoming somewhat situation-dependent in Seattle. He had thrived because the Seahawks were a winning team, which is why he saw 338 touches in 2012.

Prior to 2013, though, Lynch hadn't caught more than 28 passes in a season since 2008. It's not like he was a Michael Turner-esque receiver out of the backfield, but Lynch didn't generate a large percentage of his points as a pass-catcher. And with young pass-catching backs behind him on the Seahawks' depth chart, it stood to reason that Lynch might see a dramatic decline in usage if Seattle were to lose more games than expected.

Lynch silenced his 2013 doubters, but that doesn't mean there wasn't a certain level of volatility inherent to his game. As it turns out, pass-catching running backs have proven to be far more consistent than running backs who don't see heavy work as receivers.

Looking at all backs with at least 750 rushing yards, the top 25 percent in catches have been 14.4 percent more consistent than the bottom quarter in receptions. The typical pass-catching running back has generated 10.3 quality starts—defined the same way as with quarterbacks—per season.

Whenever you're analyzing a player, you need to envision how the course of the game could affect his production. In head-to-head leagues in which consistency is king, you want players who can produce almost regardless of the path of the contest. Someone like Reggie Bush can give you numbers even when his team is down 21 points—perhaps to an even greater degree than when they're winning—whereas a back like DeAngelo Williams can be rendered useless.

Further, because running backs who don't catch passes have limited ways to score fantasy points, they're more touchdown-dependent than pass-catching backs. Touchdowns are relatively volatile, so it makes sense to fade backs who lack versatility when you're seeking consistency.

Wide Receivers and Tight Ends

When I first started studying the week-to-week consistency of pass-catchers, I thought that receivers who are relatively dependent on big plays—think Josh Gordon or Torrey Smith—might be slightly less consistent than receivers and tight ends with shorter targets.

That's true to an extent, but what seems to matter most is the actual alignment. Receivers who play primarily in the slot have recorded over 15 percent more quality starts than those who play out wide.

Why? It's tough to say for sure. Shorter targets (and thus a higher catch rate) probably have something to do with it, but it's also more difficult to double-team a slot receiver (or a tight end). Whereas cornerbacks can use the sideline to their advantage against an X or Z receiver with safety help over the top, nickel cornerbacks need to cover slot receivers all over the field, typically without help.

Ultimately, it seems like slot receivers possess more consistency than outside receivers. That could make them quality options in the flex position for heads-up leagues, especially on full PPR sites like DraftKings.

NFL Salary Cap Allocation

When I asked DraftKings to look into their database for me, one of the topics about which I had the most excitement was salary cap allocation—how the best teams allocate their salary cap among the various positions.

Well, here's that data for head-to-head games.

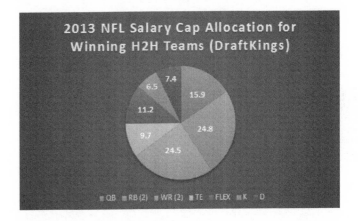

Using DraftKings' $50,000 NFL salary cap, here's how that pie chart breaks down at each position:

QB: $7,950

RB (2): $12,400 ($6,200 per)

WR (2): $12,250 ($6,125 per)

TE: $4,850

FLEX: $5,600

K: $3,250

D: $3,700

Now let's compare these numbers to those for the typical winning 50/50 lineup.

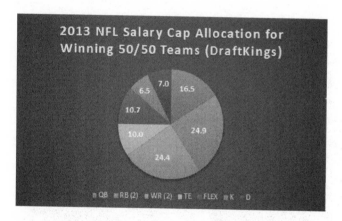

Similar, but we see more money spent at quarterback, less on the flex, and less on the defense. This could just be noise, but don't forget my previous hypothesis that many players are approaching 50/50s in the wrong way. By seeking high-upside lineups, they're increasing the value of a high floor even more.

We know that quarterbacks are consistent options from week to week, so this could be evidence that 50/50s are indeed safer than head-to-head leagues (even after adjusting for the larger sample of lineups) due to the risk-seeking manner in which many players approach 50/50s.

On a side note, it's important to mention that if you're heading into each week picking the players at each position with salaries that most closely match the percentages, you're going to be in trouble. Each week is different, so it would be foolish to bypass a specific value just because it would "mess up" your salary cap allocation.

Instead, I think the chart has value over longer periods of time. At the end of each season, analyze your lineups to see how you distributed available funds. Over larger samples, the intricacies of each individual week should even out, so your allocation should come close to resembling the average winning salary cap distribution.

If you're paying way more for a certain position than normal—say, 20 percent of your cap on quarterbacks—it might be a sign to at least analyze what you're doing to make sure you're seeing the necessary return on your investment at each position.

NFL Player Combinations

In our search for the ultimate "safe" lineup, we've covered the consistency of each position and subsets of those positions. Yet another way to increase your team's floor is to strategically pair players who are playing in the same game.

Namely, you're searching for players whose production is tied via an inverse relationship, i.e. as one player goes up, the other goes down. That doesn't necessitate one being good and the other bad, of course—they should both offer value— but the relationship between them would increase the floor of your team.

One such pairing is two starting running backs from teams facing one another. That's particularly useful in a game that could be close, as both teams would be likely to continue to run the ball throughout the game. If one of the teams gets down big and is forced to throw, however, the drop in workload you'd see from one of your backs would be offset by the increased workload from the other back.

Another pairing to consider is starting two pass-catchers in the same game. It's the same idea as with the running backs. However, you could actually start two pass-catchers on the same team, too, assuming the contest figures to be high-scoring. If you look at the Vegas line and see the Broncos-Chargers matchup with an over/under at 59 points, for example, you can be pretty sure there's going to be a whole lot of points scored. Pairing a wide receiver and tight end from the same team might not be such a poor play in a head-to-head league because, due to the relative safety of each offense as a whole, there's a solid chance that at least one (or possibly) both of the pass-catchers will go off.

You never want to combine teammates just for the sake of doing it—they always need to provide value—but creating those relationships based on your league type could increase your win probability by a few percentage points.

MLB Head-to-Head Strategy

One of the reasons I'm able to do this NFL-MLB hybrid book is because there's so much overlap between the two sports when it comes to daily fantasy. It doesn't matter if you're deciding between Drew Brees and Aaron Rodgers or Clayton Kershaw and Matt Harvey; the general principles surrounding risk and reward are the same.

So it follows that your head-to-head (or 50/50) MLB strategy is basically the same as it is in daily fantasy football: maximize your floor. Unlike in football, though, position consistency and "player types" don't matter as much because players are put in the exact same situation in baseball: 60 feet and six inches from the pitcher's mound.

You still want to seek consistency in MLB heads-up matches, but it's more about the consistency of certain stats rather than that of positions. For all practical purposes, there are two positions—hitter and pitcher—and you want to have exposure to the players who generally post more of the stats that are consistent from day to day.

MLB Scoring Data

I showed you the NFL head-to-head and 50/50 data from DraftKings. Now it's time for the MLB stats.

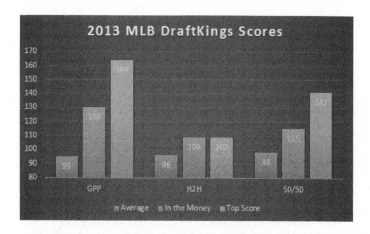

Again, the upside needed to win a GPP is obvious. Meanwhile, the average score to cash in a DraftKings MLB head-to-head is 109, compared to 115 in a 50/50. That's a significant difference and suggests that perhaps 50/50s aren't the way to go in daily fantasy baseball.

That's in contrast to what the numbers suggest in football, but why? My guess is that there are many, many daily fantasy football players who are new to daily fantasy sports. They might know football, but they don't know how to efficiently allocate cap space in the world of daily fantasy.

Daily fantasy baseball probably has more experienced players who understand how to play 50/50s, however. There's evidence of that in the average 50/50 score (98) surpassing the average head-to-head score (96); we don't see that effect in the NFL.

So it's not that there's no money to be made in daily fantasy baseball. On the contrary, the sheer number of games creates an outstanding money-making opportunity. But the new players are likely involved more with head-to-heads and GPPs than 50/50s.

Recent Play vs. Long-Term Numbers

I've talked a lot about how there's all kinds of variance in the NFL, even over the course of an entire season, because they play so few games. That variance doesn't exist over a 162-game MLB season, but it's very much in play from night to night.

On a per-game basis, there's probably even more variance in baseball stats than football stats, particularly for hitters. Whereas pitchers frequently have 100-plus opportunities to assert their dominance within the course of a single game, hitters have a rather small sample of chances to score fantasy points in a single game. A batter might swing the bat fewer than 10 times per game, and he'll rarely see more than six plate appearances to generate points. Meanwhile, quarterbacks sometimes throw the ball 50 times in a single contest.

In any random environment, we'd expect results to eventually regress toward the mean. But which mean? Are baseball players likely to regress toward their long-term mean in various statistical categories, or more probable to regress toward a recent mean, i.e. streaky play?

It appears as though there is indeed streaky play in baseball, although perhaps not to an extreme degree. We're going to see long runs of greatness and seemingly never-ending slumps because there are so many players that those events will occur just from chance alone.

However, baseball is a unique sport in that, because of the sheer volume of games, you can leverage small advantages into large ones over the course of a season. In that way, baseball is paradoxically both random and determined; it's filled with variance on the day-to-day level, but the little blips in the data even out long-term. And that's kind of what you can expect as a daily fantasy baseball player, too—ups-and-downs in the short-term, but steady long-term results.

Matt Holliday will go through all kinds of streaks and slumps within a single season, for example, but the probability of him hitting between, say, .285 and .325 at the end of the year is rather high. If we were to simulate 10,000 games for Holliday instead of 162, he'd be extremely likely to fall near his career average of .311.

When it comes down to it, we need to combine recent play with matchup data (such as the pitcher, the ballpark, the weather, and so on) *and* long-term trends. The extent to which daily fantasy players value each factor varies, but they should all be included in your analysis.

As a quick aside, I think it's worth mentioning that many daily fantasy players disagree on the value of short-term trends in MLB data, i.e. do players really get hot and cold? Again, I think they do to some degree (even if it's just an unknown injury affecting their play), but I definitely believe you should at least consider recent numbers.

The reason has to do with player salaries. Because NFL teams play just once a week, player salaries are altered a whole lot between games. Thus, players coming off of big games can be overvalued since their salary will rise, but they aren't really "hot" in any meaningful way.

That's not the case in daily fantasy baseball, though; since the teams play nearly every day, daily sites don't update the salaries so much. If streaky play exists, you should be able to obtain an advantage by considering recent stats. If it doesn't, there shouldn't be much of a disadvantage, though, since you don't need to pay more for those guys. You always want the players with optimal numbers over the long-run, but there are enough players that you can value both long-term and short-term stats.

Consistency in Head-to-Heads

My official position on "streaky" MLB play is that it probably exists, but even if it doesn't (or not to an extreme degree), it probably doesn't hurt you to value short-term stats, assuming long-term stats are still the backbone of your research. Almost all successful daily fantasy baseball players will tell you to emphasize large samples of data and then adjust for recent trends, not the other way around.

Mike5754—one of the premiere MLB players in daily fantasy—is one of those players.

"I tend to use numbers from huge samples. I don't even look at BvP (batter vs. pitcher) data, for example. I just care about a guy's numbers against lefties or righties, for the most part, because the BvP stuff is so dependent on the situation.

Also, I tend to value a player's career numbers over recent stats. You can get fooled by a single game or even a stretch of games, but the numbers mean something after a few seasons. All of those subjective factors even out.

So over the first month of the season, for example, I use only stats from the past three years. After that, I slowly include the numbers from the current season, but I still value primarily the long-term data."

This is important information when searching for consistency because we need to know which stats are the most reliable. Regardless of the importance you place on streaky play versus data from larger samples, it's important to know the consistency of each stat.

Studying Year-to-Year Trends

I collected data on the season-to-season consistency of various individual player stats. Why not game-to-game consistency? Remember, baseball's consistency is easily apparent over large stretches of games, but not so obvious over the course of a single game, week, or even month.

You might be saying "Uh, yeah, idiot, so if there's no consistency from game to game, why even look at the numbers?"

First of all, watch your language. Second, it's not that there's *zero* consistent from game to game, but just that it's minute enough that we can't really detect it or separate it from randomness. But we know it must be there since there's all kinds of consistency from year to year.

And in daily fantasy baseball, small advantages can equal big profit down the line. By continually placing yourself at the right end of the consistency spectrum, you can turn a minor positive into an enormous advantage over the course of a season.

Batter Consistency Data

So here it is—the year-to-year consistency of various hitting stats.

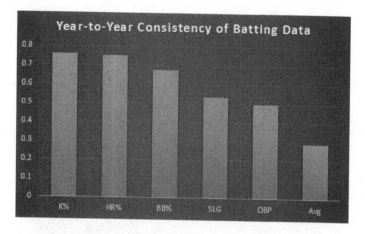

The two most reliable hitting stats are strikeout percentage and home run percentage. The strikeout percentage is understandable given the number of Ks in each game, but the home run percentage is less expected, at least to me.

There were 18,336 total strikeouts during the 2013 baseball season, but only 2,504 home runs—over seven strikeouts per long ball. Even as a relatively low-frequency event, though, home runs have been about as consistent as strikeouts—the power of a large sample size.

CSURAM88 agrees with this approach. "I pay for home runs for batters. It doesn't matter what league type, I like to look at 3-4-5-6 hitters who can hit for power in any game."

Meanwhile, walks carry over from one season to the next at a higher rate than average. There's more evidence of that in the slugging percentage (SLG) and on-base percentage (OBP) correlations, which are in many ways a hybrid of the other stats on here.

Pitcher Consistency Data

And now for the pitchers. . .

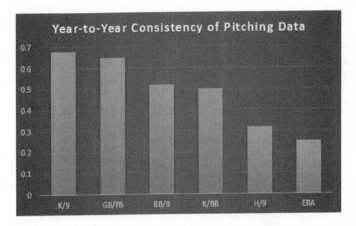

As is the case with hitters, strikeouts are the most consistent stats for pitchers. The coefficient of determination for strikeouts per nine innings is 0.68. Groundballs per fly ball is the next most consistent major stat for pitchers—even more so than walks or hits per nine innings—which is mildly surprising.

Not shockingly, ERA is the least consistent major stat for pitchers with an R-Squared of only 0.25—lower than the value for batting average.

How to Use the Numbers in Heads-Up Games

The reason that consistency stats matter is because your projections are only as useful as the ability of the numbers to carry over from one game, one week, or one year to the next. Even if you knew beyond a shadow of a doubt that one pitcher would throw a perfect game in a given night, the information would be useless to you if there were no predictability in pitcher stats from night to night. The more comfortable you can be in your predictions—the more consistency inherent to certain stats—the more weight you can place on your projections.

When trying to increase the floor of your daily fantasy baseball team in a head-to-head matchup, you want to pay for the stats that 1) give you the most points and 2) are the most likely to remain consistent.

To give you an idea of that process, let's take a look at part of DraftKings' MLB scoring. DraftKings awards 10 points for a home run and two points for a walk. If we want to project, say, Albert Pujols in both categories on a given night, we might start with his career baseline averages of 0.25 home runs per night and 0.54 walks.

Right off the bat, you're looking at 2.5 projected points from home runs and 1.08 points from walks. But the disparity between the two stats is even greater because home runs have been a bit more consistent than walks from year to year (a coefficient of determination of 0.75 versus 0.68).

You could simply multiply the projected points by the consistency correlations to obtain an adjusted projection of 1.88 for home runs (2.5 * 0.75) and 0.73 for walks (1.08 * 0.68).

Now, I don't think the math is necessary when projecting every player each day, but the broader picture is more valuable: in head-to-head matchups, you want to pay for the players and stats that are most likely to get you points, thus increasing your floor projection.

For hitters, you might want to consider home runs as a more consistent source of production than previously thought. Any single player is probably unlikely to hit a homer in a given night, but the odds of your entire lineup knocking a few out of the park can be decent. And as the season progresses, that little advantage will accumulate into a bigger one.

Meanwhile, you're probably better off not paying up for guys who 1) don't hit for power and/or 2) don't walk a lot. Drawing walks is a pretty consistent skill, so it holds more value in heads-up matches than tournaments. Hitting for power is even more important.

Contrary to popular belief, players like Salvador Perez who hit for average but don't have an exorbitant number of walks or home runs probably aren't as consistent (relative to their salary) as some other batters. Even a player like Joe Mauer, despite a decent number of walks, is probably overvalued on most occasions.

For pitchers, it's all about the Ks. On DraftKings, pitchers get just 0.5 points less for one strikeout (2 points) than they do for a complete game (2.5 points). Just two strikeouts equals one win (4 points). Because strikeouts are 1) a big contributor to total points, 2) consistent, and 3) scarce (meaning some pitchers have a lot more than others), they're very valuable in head-to-head leagues.

MLB Salary Cap Allocation

As was the case with their NFL data, DraftKings hooked me up with the salary cap allocation of winning MLB teams. Here you go.

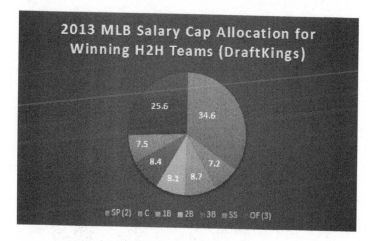

With two starting pitcher spots, winning head-to-head lineups spend an average of 17.3 percent of their cap space on each pitcher. You can see that they're typically saving at catcher and shortstop, which is to be expected. The typical winning head-to-head lineup pays an average of 8.5 percent of his cap on each outfielder.

Now, let's compare that to the typical 50/50 distribution.

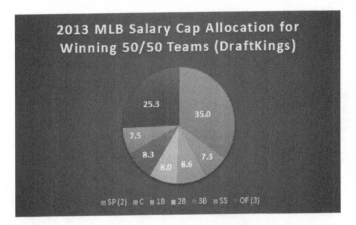

As expected, the allocation is similar to that for winning head-to-head lineups. The average 50/50 winner is actually spending slightly more on starting pitchers, though, and slightly less on outfielders. Many pros will tell you that paying for starting pitching is the safe move in head-to-head and 50/50s.

MLB Player Combinations

Just as in football, there are some player relationships in baseball that are connected via an inverse relationship (such as batter vs. pitcher). If you start a bunch of batters and the pitcher they're facing, chances are your hitters will stink if your pitcher has a decent outing.

But here's the difference between football and baseball, and it's an important one: baseball stats are zero-sum and football stats aren't. By that, I mean that if your pitcher gets points, the hitter loses points, and vice versa.

In football, on the other hand, you can comfortably start wide receivers facing one another. Their play is connected, of course, but when one scores, it doesn't cut into the other's fantasy points. You never want to create a situation in which playing one guy will actually have a negative impact on another's performance within your lineup. That relationship reduces both your ceiling and floor.

The 10 Laws of Head-to-Head (and 50/50) Strategy

Head-to-head and 50/50 leagues are so important because they're low-risk propositions that can provide a steady return. Let's run through the 10 most important points from this chapter.

Law No. 1: Head-to-head and 50/50s should be the foundation of your league structure.

Any league that pays out a high percentage of entrants will offer you a more consistent return on your money. So even if tournaments provide the best long-term ROI, it can take a long time to see that money make its way back into your account (depending on the type of GPPs you enter). That makes head-to-head leagues and 50/50s perhaps the best practical investment choice.

Law No. 2: Enter as many NFL 50/50s and MLB head-to-heads as your bankroll will allow.

While entering a single lineup into 50/50s is risky, the data suggests that, because daily fantasy football players are approaching them with the wrong strategy, they're perhaps better investments than head-to-head leagues. As long as you aren't compromising the integrity of your bankroll, 50/50s are outstanding investments in daily fantasy football.

That might not be the case in daily fantasy baseball, and it probably has something to do with the type of people who are playing the game. There are still lots of novices, i.e. "bad money," but they don't seem to be playing as many 50/50s.

Law No. 3: You should vary head-to-head and 50/50s based on your player pool.

The primary factor that should dictate how much of your bankroll you place into 50/50s versus heads-up leagues is the number of potential players you're willing to use in a given night or weekend. If you like relatively few players, you should stick with head-to-heads since you won't be able to vary your lineups too much. If you've assigned a bunch of players with near the same values, though, you can enter more 50/50s with a "diversified portfolio."

Law No. 4: Your goal in both league types is increase your floor.

Your goal in a head-to-head is the same as in a 50/50—play it safe. Do everything in your power to increase the floor of your team. You don't need a 190-point night in a 50/50; 150 points will usually do the trick.

Law No. 5: In NFL, you can play it safe by paying for quarterbacks and running backs.

Quarterbacks and running backs are far more consistent than every other position on a weekly basis. That's likely due to the number of plays in which they're primary contributors: 30-plus for quarterbacks and 15-plus for starting running backs, as compared to far fewer for wide receivers and tight ends.

When you're valuing safety, you should allocate a higher percentage of your cap to the least volatile positions. The numbers show that the best NFL head-to-head and 50/50 lineups typically pay a healthy amount for quarterbacks and running backs.

Law No. 6: In MLB, you should pay for consistent stats like home runs and strikeouts.

In the same way that you pay for consistent positions in daily fantasy football, you want to emphasize safe stats in baseball. Paying for home runs (yes, home runs!) for hitters and strikeouts for pitchers is a smart way to maximize your team's floor over the long run.

Law No. 7: Target certain types of NFL players who display week-to-week consistency.

In addition to specific positions, there are certain types of players who have proven to be the most consistent from week to week: mobile quarterbacks, pass-catching running backs, and slot receivers. When possible, favor those position archetypes in leagues that require safety.

Law No. 8: Target quality starting pitching.

Most pros will tell you that they pay for starting pitchers in head-to-head leagues. That's not a coincidence, because the data suggests that pitchers are far more reliable than hitters from game to game.

Law No. 9: Always pay attention to long-term MLB trends.

While you should certainly take note of recent trends—baseball players have a higher probability of "getting hot" than football players, after all—you also need to be aware of long-term trends. If you're projecting a player in a given night, chances are the best projection will be the one that most effectively combines his historic stats with those in recent nights or weeks.

Law No. 10: Avoid volatile player combinations.

In the NFL, playing a quarterback with his receiver is a good way to increase volatility—something you don't want in a head-to-head league. Instead, search for players whose production is connected via an inverse relationship, such as two running backs in the same game but on different teams. In baseball, filling every hitter slot with players on the same MLB team can also increase risk since they need to hit against the same pitcher.

"My theory is to strive for consistency, not to worry about the numbers. If you dwell on statistics, you get shortsighted. If you aim for consistency, the numbers will be there at the end."

- *Tom Seaver*

4 You Down With GPPs!? How to Win Tournaments

"Why not go out on a limb? That's where the fruit is."

- *Will Rogers*

When people hear the word 'risk,' it seems to conjure a bad feeling in the pits of their stomachs. Even for me—someone who most would consider pretty risk-seeking—the word doesn't sit well. Risk. Woof.

But there's a major difference between taking a risk for the pure thrill of it—which can be fun if not a sound long-term strategy—and taking a calculated risk because it's the intelligent thing to do. You can play daily fantasy sports however you'd like, but if you want to increase your upside while ensuring that you stay in the game, you need to take risks of the calculated variety—those that increase your long-term expected value.

GPPs—guaranteed prize pools—and other tournaments in which a relatively low percentage of entrants can cash generally possess a higher level of risk than other league types. On many daily fantasy sites, you might see only one-in-20 players finish in the money.

But many tournaments also offer the best long-term money-making opportunity. Let me give you an idea why that's the case.

My Uncle Bruce started to play daily fantasy football this year. He calls me from time to time for lineup advice, so I ask what leagues he's entering. And the answer is pretty much the same every time: "Oh, I'm entering DraftKings' Sunday 200 Grand. I'm also trying to qualify for the Millionaire Grand Final. Oh yeah, I'll be in the $50K Hail Mary this week, too."

Surprise, surprise. The 50-year old king of beef jerky who's still learning the daily fantasy ropes wants to win a whole lot of money at once. And guess what? There are a whole lot more Uncle Bruce's out there. You want to face those players as much as possible (Side note: Bruce reads my books, so this is going to end up being super awkward).

In a perfect world, we'd have a bankroll large enough to ensure that we could enter enough tournaments to see a return on our investment. Since that's not the case for Uncle Bruce and it's probably not the case for you, either, you'll need to do everything in your power to eliminate the risk of tournaments while maintaining the high ceiling.

DraftKings Tourneys

Here's the No. 1 way to eliminate some of the downside of tournaments: play them at DraftKings. Before I contacted DraftKings to do this book, I transferred pretty much my entire bankroll there because of the tournament structure.

In almost every large league, you're looking at a one-in-four or one-in-five shot as cashing. In a league that pays out the top 25 percent, that's a 50 percent chance of cashing if you enter four leagues and a 75 percent probability of seeing a return if you enter eight leagues. With entry levels as low as a quarter (a QUARTER!), you can very quickly eliminate much of the risk associated with tournaments.

Assuming you have exposure to the right players, you can generate sustainable profits in these tournaments without much risk but all of the upside. It's basically like playing in 50/50 or triple-ups, but an elite score will result in a whole lot more cash.

Variance

As I've mentioned, one of the aspects of daily fantasy sports that you need to grasp in any league type, but especially tournaments, is variance. There's little doubt that daily fantasy sports are games of skill—there's a reason a lot of the same names continually find themselves atop the leaderboards—but it would be a mistake to play as if you'll *always* win, no matter who you are.

In tournaments, regardless of the payout structure, the single-lineup variance is greater than in a head-to-head league. Remember how head-to-head lineups become safer as you enter more leagues (because you face a wider range of scores) but 50/50 lineups become more volatile as you enter more leagues?

Well, tournaments are like 50/50s (or triple-ups, or any type of multiplier like that); if you enter the same lineup again and again, you're creating volatility. And some daily fantasy players actually covet that. Some of the best will often submit the same lineup into multiple tournaments, GPPs, and (especially) qualifiers in a true "go big or go home" approach.

But most avoid that strategy because it holds unparalleled risk. Yes, you could absolutely crush the lineup on your way to an amazing day, but that's far from the most-likely scenario. So for us mortals, it's crucial to make sure we have enough deviation in our lineups to hedge against a poor week.

Tournament Lineup Structure

As was the recommended strategy in 50/50s, you need to strike a balance between lineup deviation and implementing the optimal plays. Remember, as you increase the pool from which you're willing to draw players, you're also necessarily selecting guys who are worse than those who came before them. As the player pool becomes larger, your potential profitability does the opposite.

Still, I typically prefer a larger player pool (especially for tournaments) than most involved in daily fantasy, for two reasons. First, it increases safety. Entering a bunch of different lineups into tournaments allows you to 1) increase your chances of winning, obviously, and 2) decrease the probability of a debilitating week. In short, it keeps you in the game.

Second, and more important, most daily fantasy players' largest weakness is failing to account for the fact that they can't make perfect predictions. They project players to score a certain number of points based on a variety of factors (which I'll touch on in the next chapter), which is fine, but then they select just a handful of the top values as if their projections are flawless.

Because there are so many different players in both NFL and MLB in a given day, though, you'll find that you typically have a whole bunch of guys projected near one another. If you increase a second-tier wide receiver by 15 yards or a third-tier pitcher by one strikeout, it can completely throw off your rankings and values.

That's a fragile strategy. If you can truly project a wide receiver within 15 yards of his output on a consistent basis, you sure don't need to be reading this book. You have millions of dollars to go make.

But you can't, so I guess you have to read on.

It's not that creating projections or player values is useless, but just that if you don't account for the fact that you're probably not as good at doing it as you think you are, you're going to end up with an unnecessarily small player pool that's perhaps (but perhaps not) marginally better than a larger player pool.

That's why I recommend utilizing more players and worrying more about your total exposure to each player. You should put your top values in the most lineups, your second-tier values in a few less, and so on. You shouldn't expand the number of players you're willing to start to such a great degree that you'll play almost anyone, but using a tiered approach with more options decreases risk in tournaments and accounts for the fact that, hey, you might be a teeny tiny bit wrong at times.

Break Through the Ceiling

In tournaments, a mediocre score isn't going to do you much good. You need greatness, so median player projections are basically worthless. You must know each player's ceiling—the maximum possible points he could score—and how likely he is to reach that ceiling.

One way to do that is to understand the position and individual stat consistency numbers from the previous chapter. If you know that there's a more linear relationship between running back points or pitcher strikeouts and their salaries than there is between wide receiver points or a pitcher's hits allowed and their salaries, that can be used in all different league types.

Unlike in head-to-head leagues, though, you actually want to seek volatility in tournaments. You want those boom-or-bust players in your lineup—the wide receiver who could give you next to nothing or could explode for 150 yards and two touchdowns (Hi Mike Wallace!).

If you're examining the NFL consistency stats, for example, you'll find that top wide receivers are far less consistent than running backs from week to week. That means wide receiver's points tend to come in bunches—there's a pretty big deviation between their best weeks and worst weeks—so they'll typically have higher ceilings (relative to their average level of production) than the backs (especially on full PPR sites like DraftKings).

So for tournaments, GPPs, qualifiers, and other large-field leagues that pay out a relatively small portion of entrants, you should be using a "Britney Spears approach," sacrificing stability and consistency for volatility, knowing that when you're on, you'll be *really* on.

As I mentioned in Chapter 1, one quick and easy way to generate ceiling projections for the NFL is with the rotoViz GLSP app. The app collects data on the matchup similar to the one you're studying, providing 25 comparable players facing similar defenses. It also provides you a low, median, and high projection for each player based on his comps.

Drew Brees vs DAL

Projection

-	4 Pt PTD	6 Pt PTD
Low	16.9	19.4
Median	21.5	27.5
High	29	36.2

Contributing Matchups

Name	SEAS	WK	DEF	ATTS	COMP	YDS	Y/A	PTDS	INTS	RYDS	RTDS
Drew Brees	2011	12	NYG	38	24.00	363	9.55	4	0	8	1
Drew Brees	2012	15	TB	39	26.00	306	7.85	4	0	11	0
Drew Brees	2012	1	WAS	52	24.00	338	6.50	3	2	0	0
Peyton Manning	2012	13	TB	38	27.00	242	6.37	3	1	-2	0
Matthew Stafford	2011	12	GB	45	32.00	276	6.13	1	3	31	0
Drew Brees	2012	7	TB	37	27.00	376	10.16	4	1	1	0
Peyton Manning	2012	8	NO	30	22.00	305	10.17	3	0	4	0
Tom Brady	2011	4	OAK	30	16.00	226	7.53	2	0	-1	0
Drew Brees	2011	1	GB	49	32.00	418	8.53	3	0	3	0
Tom Brady	2011	9	NYG	49	28.00	340	6.94	2	2	5	0
Matt Ryan	2012	12	TB	32	26.00	353	11.03	1	1	13	0
Matt Ryan	2012	17	TB	44	28.00	238	5.41	1	0	11	0
Tony Romo	2012	3	TB	39	25.00	283	7.26	0	1	6	0
Matt Ryan	2012	13	NO	33	18.00	165	5.00	1	0	-3	0
Matt Ryan	2012	5	WAS	52	34.00	345	6.63	2	1	2	0
Drew Brees	2011	13	DET	36	26.00	342	9.50	3	0	0	0
Matt Ryan	2012	10	NO	52	34.00	411	7.90	3	1	2	0
Tony Romo	2012	17	WAS	37	20.00	218	5.89	2	3	0	0
Matthew Stafford	2011	17	GB	59	36.00	520	8.81	5	2	0	0
Matthew Stafford	2011	15	OAK	52	29.00	391	7.52	4	0	5	0
Tony Romo	2012	16	NO	43	26.00	415	9.65	4	0	0	0
Matt Schaub	2009	11	TEN	39	25.00	304	7.79	2	0	0	0
Rich Gannon	2002	17	KC	14	7.00	79	5.64	1	0	3	0
Peyton Manning	2012	5	NE	44	31.00	345	7.84	3	0	9	0
Aaron Rodgers	2012	4	NO	41	31.00	319	7.78	4	1	14	0

Whereas the median projection is significant to you in head-to-head leagues, all that matters in tournaments is the high projection.

As a quick aside, note that it's never a good idea to pay a lot for a position like kicker, even though they're volatile. One reason is that there's no individual predictability there; whereas you can use matchups and other data to predict individual wide receiver performances, that's of relatively little importance for kickers. Second, there's little scarcity inherent to the position. What's the maximum number of points that the top kicker can get you over an average kicker? Probably like 15. Meanwhile, Calvin Johnson can go for 50 points at any time.

Stacking the Deck

Some people are naturally better heads-up players than tournament gurus, but I find myself in the latter category. I've kind of built my entire life around enhancing and realizing upside—I'd rather make $20k a year with the chance at millions over a guaranteed $80k salary—so that mentality lends itself nicely to tournaments.

If upside is what you crave, the manner in which you structure your lineups will be of the utmost importance to you. Namely, you want to create dependent relationships without your lineup—situations through which the superiority of one player increases the probability of another player (or multiple players) producing for you (and, on the flip side, the shitty play of one decrease the odds of production from others).

When you enter a GPP or qualifier that pays out a small percentage of entrants, it doesn't matter if you have a score in the 30th percentile—you need great, not just good—so your goal should really be to shoot for the moon. That will increase both the ceiling and floor of your team, which is a positive when you need to hit a home run (or, in the case of MLB tournaments, *many* home runs). The act of pairing teammates to increase upside is known as "stacking" in the world of daily fantasy sports.

When playing daily fantasy football, you can increase upside by pairing your quarterback with one of his receivers. If the quarterback has a big day, which is pretty much a prerequisite for taking down a tourney, it's highly likely that your pass-catcher will produce as well. Take a look at the strong correlation between quarterback points and team wide receiver points.

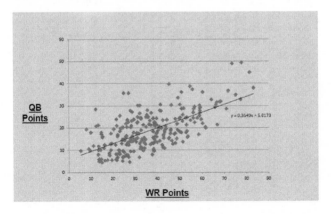

When a quarterback has at least 30 points on DraftKings, there's roughly a 91.7 percent chance that his wide receivers will combine for 30 or more points, an 83.3 percent chance of them checking in above 40 points, a two-in-three probability of 50-plus points, and incredibly a one-in-three chance of at least 70 combined points.

In daily fantasy baseball, the production of teammates is perhaps even more strongly correlated. When a hitter goes off, it's just as likely that it was because of his own ability as it was that the pitcher just sucked. And when the pitcher sucks, guess what? Everyone is putting up numbers.

So there are a bunch of different ways to structure your lineups in both NFL and MLB to maximize upside. Which are the best ones? Let's dig into the data.

NFL Tournament Data

You need to hit on the majority of your players in most tournaments, obviously, but what kind of floor is there on a player tanking? Well, check out the average high and low scores for winning daily fantasy football lineups on DraftKings.

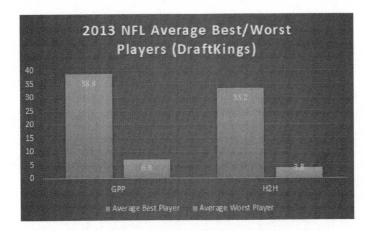

In the typical head-to-head matchup, the winner has a high-scoring player of 33.2 points and a low-scoring player of 3.8 points. For GPPs, however, the respective averages are 38.8 and 6.8 points.

That low-scoring player is perhaps more important than the top dog because it shows just how important it is to hit on each pick in a tournament. Whereas the typical highest-scoring player in a head-to-head is 85.6 percent of that in a tourney, the average lowest-scoring player in a heads-up is only 55.9 percent of his low-scoring tournament counterpart.

Paying for Volatile Players

As with head-to-head matchups, you want to seek certain types of players in tournaments. Instead of consistency, though, you want to favor those players whose production is volatile from week to week. I already mentioned you can do that by paying for the least consistent positions (up to a point) and using player comps to generate ceiling projections.

You can also seek volatility by targeting players whose production is relatively fluky. Remember how mobile quarterbacks and pass-catching running backs are valuable in head-to-head games because they have high floors? Well, big-play backs and receivers are valuable in large-field leagues because they're volatile options—dependent on big plays for production.

And the biggest predictor of big-play ability, as you might have guessed, is speed. So while players like Frank Gore and Wes Welker might be awesome heads-up and 50/50 options because of their consistency, it's the Chris Johnson and C.J. Spiller-esque "black swan" players who often lead to tournament victories.

You can get all kinds of data on big plays at Pro Football Focus (such as deep targets, percentage of yards from big plays, and so on).

NFL Salary Cap Allocation

As with head-to-head leagues, I received data from DraftKings in regards to the optimal salary cap allocation in tournaments. Here it is.

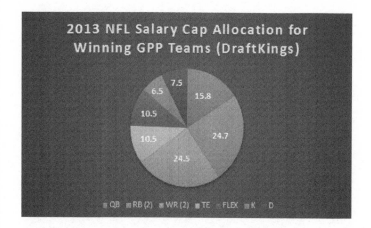

Want to hear a funny story? Well, you're shit out of luck, because I just have a regular story...not funny in the least, but a story nonetheless.

I began writing this book, including much of this chapter, before I received all of the data from DraftKings. I wrote only the sections that I could without the numbers, and this particular salary cap allocation data was really important to the chapter. It's just really unique stuff you won't find anywhere else.

Anyway, much of the premise of my tournament strategy is that it makes sense to pay for a little volatility in tournaments since you need upside. That includes perhaps paying more for wide receivers and tight ends—the positions we've deemed as the least consistent (of the main four) from week to week.

So to be honest, I was going to have to re-write thousands of words here if these numbers came in differently. Luckily, my hunch was confirmed; paying for consistency isn't nearly as valuable in GPPs as it is in head-to-head or 50/50 leagues.

Looking at the GPP salary cap pie chart, here's how the positions break down in regards to DraftKings' $50,000 cap. The numbers in parentheses indicate how the salaries compare to those for the typical winning 50/50 lineup.

QB: $7,900 (-$350)

RB (2): $12,350 (-$100)

WR (2): $12,250 (+$50)

TE: $5,250 (+$250)

FLEX: $5,250 (-$100)

K: $3,250 (Same)

D: $3,750 (+$250)

Considering the number of lineups analyzed in this study, these differences are very significant. It's no surprise that winning GPP lineups pay more money for pass-catchers (who also have higher upside in full PPR leagues) by saving cap space at quarterback and running back—the exact opposite of the optimal head-to-head and 50/50 strategy.

Also note that winning GPPs spend more money on defenses. At $250 more per pop compared to 50/50s, that's a really big jump and evidence that going "off the map" a little can be advantageous in tournaments.

NFL Player Combinations

So you've entered a big qualifier and you've decided to stack a quarterback and wide receiver. Nice move. But what about another one of their teammates? Does it make sense to stack a quarterback with two of his pass-catchers?

The answer is "it depends." Namely, it depends on the league type. In a huge GPP with thousands of players, you need massive upside. In that case, a QB-WR-WR pairing (or QB-WR-TE) will limit some of your upside. If your quarterback has a huge day, it's fairly likely that both of your receivers will have, say, top 20 days. Maybe one will even be a top two or three player at his position.

But it's not that likely that *both* receivers will have elite outings because each catch, yard, and touchdown for one means the other gets nothing. So the probability of both players recording a top five day, which you need to win a huge tourney, is pretty slim.

If you're in a big-but-not-so-big-that-I-can't-even-count-that-high sort of league, however (one with 100 entrants, for example), you can get away with a QB-WR-WR strategy. In such a format, you need lots of upside, but not so much so that you can't pair pass-catchers on the same team. It's particularly smart to use a QB-WR-WR strategy on a team projected by Vegas to score a boatload of points.

Another player combination that increases your upside—one that I termed "anti-stacking" in my last book—is pairing a quarterback (and/or a receiver or two) with a running back that's playing in the same game, but on the opposite team. If the Steelers are facing the Bengals and you're using Le'Veon Bell, for example, it would be wise to pair him with Andy Dalton in a tournament. If Bell goes off, chances are the Steelers would be winning the game—a scenario that would cause Cincy to air it out often, helping Dalton & Co.

There are of course player combos to avoid in tournaments, too, such as two running backs playing in the same game. You should also bypass a quarterback and running back on the same team, unless you're talking about a Reggie Bush or Darren Sproles-type back whose fantasy points often come via the pass.

MLB Tournament Data

I already showed you the distribution of scores in head-to-heads, 50/50s, and GPPs in the last chapter. Now, let's take a look at the average best and worst player in winning MLB lineups.

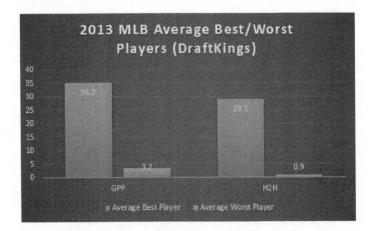

There's no surprise here, but it shows you exactly how much upside you need in MLB tournaments. The highest-scoring player is typically over six points higher than in a head-to-head, but check out the lowest-scoring player. If you plan to take down a GPP or even cash in it, any negative score is going to ruin your chances.

So how can you maximize the probability of a killer GPP lineup? Let's check out the salary cap allocation for the winning teams.

MLB Salary Cap Allocation
Again, this is the typical distribution of funds solely for those lineups that have *won* MLB tournaments.

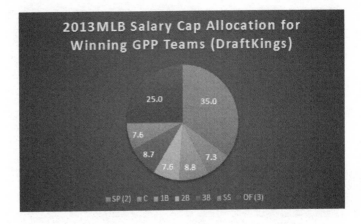

Again, the results are close to those from winning head-to-head and 50/50 leagues because of the massive sample. Here's how these numbers break down by salary, based on DraftKings' $50,000 cap. The numbers in parentheses represent the change from the typical 50/50 distribution.

SP (2): $17,500 (Same)

C: $3,650 (Same)

1B: $4,400 (+$100)

2B: $3,800 (-$200)

3B: $4,350 (+$200)

SS: $3,800 (+$50)

OF (3): $12,500 (-$150)

The best GPP lineups are paying slightly more for shortstops, first basemen and third basemen, and a bit less for second basemen and outfielders. Meanwhile, they continue to pay up for pitchers.

I want to take this time to use pitchers as an example of why less risk doesn't necessarily equate to less reward. In tournaments, what you're really looking to do is identify potentially large deviations in production and exploit them. That's why you should never pay up for a kicker in football; in addition to no predictability, there's also little deviation in their points.

Starting pitchers have the ability to offer consistency (due to their workloads in each game) *and* high ceilings (because of the potential deviation in points from the best to the worst). That's why, even in tournaments in which you'll likely pair teammates to increase upside, you should focus on building around your pitchers. Just because the best ones are safe doesn't mean they don't also offer GPP-worthy upside.

MLB Player Combinations (Stacking)

MLB players aren't dependent on one another in the same way as NFL players, but they are highly dependent on sub-par play from the opponent. Namely, pitchers benefit from facing an offense of struggling hitters. To a much larger degree, the play of batters on the same team is very strongly correlated due to facing the same pitchers.

Just as pairing a quarterback and wide receiver increases your upside, so does combining baseball players on the same team. Stacking multiple hitters is at least a moderately risky move because there's a good chance that the majority of them will either give you great numbers or just tank.

That makes stacking a strategy that's smart—crucial, even—in tournaments. But how many players is optimal?

I actually wrote part of this section before all of the DraftKings data was available, and here is what I had to say:

> *And just as in daily fantasy football, the number of players you stack will determine your floor and ceiling. If you're competing in a huge GPP, for example, you don't want to stack an entire team of hitters because 1) you'll likely need to play sub-optimal values to do that and 2) it's very unlikely they'll all go off, even if the pitcher has a horrible game. Sticking with two and three-team stacks (all hitters from two or three MLB teams) is the way to go.*

The main reason I think this book will really help daily fantasy players is that I'm trying to throw all preconceived notions out the window and use hard data to determine the true best course of action in different situations.

And guess what? That paragraph on stacking was completely wrong! Here's why.

Stacking your entire team (or close to it) with players from
the same MLB team dramatically increases your upside. I
charted the probability of scoring 150-plus point based on the
number of players from the same MLB team in your lineup.

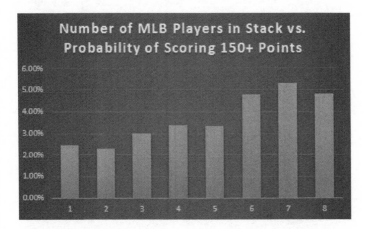

While the odds of scoring 150-plus points (and the probability
of winning a large GPP) are just 2.45 percent for teams
without any sort of stack, that percentage peaks at 5.32
percent for seven-player stacks. That means you can increase
your probability of taking down a tournament by stacking
seven players by 2.17 times what it would be without any
stack.

Let me repeat that: MLB lineups with seven-player stacks
have scored 150-plus points over twice as often as those
without any stacking. Actually, seven-player stacks have
significantly outperformed four and five-man stacks, too,
both of which lead to 150-plus points less than 3.40 percent
of the time.

The big jump comes at the six-player mark, meaning you really, really need to consider implementing six, seven, or even eight-man stacks when playing in large leagues.

If you really like two different teams of MLB hitters in a night, you can certainly consider two four-man stacks, but make sure the hitters are near one another in the batting order (a group of 3-4-5-6 hitters, for example). Their play is correlated since they'll face the same pitcher, but they offer way more upside than, say, a 1-2-6-8 combination of hitters, without significantly more risk. That's because hitters who are near each other in the order can give you multiple points on the same play; a two-RBI double on which you have both baserunners and the hitter can be awfully valuable.

So we know that stacking increases upside to such a degree that you seriously need to consider full-team stacks in large leagues, but what's the downside? As you'd imagine, stacking is risky. Check out how many DraftKings lineups have finished with fewer than 50 points based on the number of players they stacked.

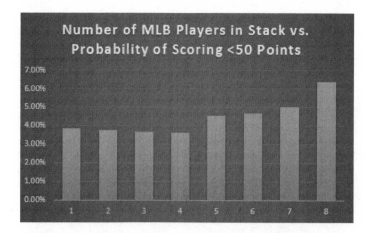

There's certainly a lot of risk with heavy-stacks; eight-man stacks finish with fewer than 50 points 6.38 percent of the time, whereas that happens to only 3.86 percent of the time for teams that aren't stacked at all.

But there are two reasons to suggest that stacking might very well be a superior play in head-to-head matchups than what we previously considered. First, the deviation in risk isn't nearly as great as that in upside. Whereas there's a dramatic difference between two and seven-man stacks in regards to scoring 150 points, there's not too much of a deviation in terms of risk; a seven-man stack is just 30 percent more likely to finish with a score below 50 points than a team that doesn't stack at all. When you weigh the upside, the value of stacking is obvious.

Second, and more important, there's actually slightly *less* risk in stacking four players than not stacking anyone! Thus, the safest lineup you could roll out could very well be a pair of three/four-man stacks.

That's reflected in this chart showing the percentage of teams to finish with at least 90 points DraftKings.

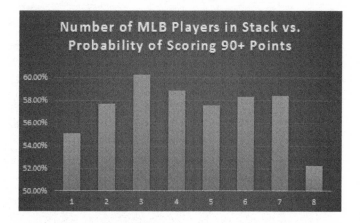

This is an awesome combination of the previous data. When you're looking for safety in a head-to-head or 50/50, you actually don't want to play hitters from eight separate teams. Actually, the only stack that's worse than no stack (in terms of safety) is an eight-man stack.

So unlike in football—a sport in which stacking players can truly increase variance—you should be looking to stack in *all MLB league types*. That's not a popular opinion, but it's one that the data suggests is true. If possible, look to use near full-team stacks in large GPPs and a pair of three/four-man stacks in smaller leagues.

And since few daily fantasy players are stacking teams in heads-up and 50/50 leagues, it could provide a substantial competitive advantage.

Finding the Right Stacks

While the pros have slightly different views on targeting pitchers or hitters first in tournaments, the process for identifying the right stacks is the same: look at the Vegas lines, narrow down your search to offenses facing struggling pitchers, consider how the individual hitters perform versus lefties/righties, and finally analyze factors such as the ballpark, weather, umpire, and so on.

The highly ranked daily fantasy player 'Notorious' took me through his process. "I check the over/under for each game to see who Vegas thinks will score a lot of runs. I'll have a group of potential teams to stack, and then I narrow those down by looking at how the offenses do against either lefties or righties, depending on the opposing pitcher.

After that, I'll have a few possible stacks. Depending on the tournament, I might use all of them, or I might differentiate among them based on other factors. The ballpark is a big one. Some stadiums are friendly to hitters, and others favor pitchers.

I also look at wind speed a lot, because if it's really blowing in hard, I'll fade that team in tournaments. There are certain stadiums like Wrigley field where it can get windy and that totally changes the projected runs. Sometimes it can move by two runs or more if it's really windy, so that's an obviously important factor."

Considering the DraftKings data from the previous section, it's pretty clear that hitting on the right hitter stacks is important, regardless of the league type you're entering.

Being a Contrarian

Ever hear of the Monty Hall problem? Here's a quick synopsis.

You're on a game show and you're allowed to choose one of three doors in order to win a prize. There's a new car behind one of the doors, but nothing (or a goat, or a hamburger, or whatever) behind the other two doors. So right out of the gate, you have a 33 percent chance to pick the car.

You choose Door No. 1. The host, who knows where the car is located, opens up Door No. 3 to show you one of the goats. He then asks you if you'd like to switch your selection to Door No. 2. Should you do it?

According to polls, most people wouldn't switch and think that doing so wouldn't change their odds of being correct. The truth is that you should switch your selection every time. While it initially seems like you can't increase your probability of being correct by switching—that it was one-in-three to start and it's still one-in-three after the game show host shows you what's behind one of the doors—that's not correct.

The key to the problem is the host's knowledge of the game. Since he knows where the car is located, he will only open one of the other doors. With that in mind, you can actually double your probability of winning if you switch.

There are three possible locations for the car. If it's behind Door No. 1 and you switch to Door No. 2, you'll lose. If it's behind Door No. 2, you'll win. And if it were behind Door No. 3—and this is the key—the host wouldn't have opened that door. Instead, he would have opened Door. No 2, and you would have the option to switch to Door No. 3 to win it.

So by switching, you actually have a two-in-three chance to win the car instead of one-in-three. And the key is the host's knowledge of the game, which many people overlook.

I added that because it's a cool thought experiment with results many find shocking and sometimes don't believe even after explanation. But it also has some implications on daily fantasy sports. Namely, the game theory you must implement in order to astutely switch your choice is also necessary in your tournament play.

Specifically, it can sometimes be intelligent to avoid extremely obvious value plays in tournaments if you have a hunch that most others will use that same player. Suppose you're filling out a GPP lineup and Eddie Lacy stands out as a value—so clear that you'd be shocked if he's not in 40 percent of all lineups in the tournament.

Naturally, it seems like you need him in your lineup. And that would definitely be the case if you were in a heads-up or 50/50 league because you could never be sure your opponent would use Lacy and it really wouldn't matter all that much if he did.

But in a tourney, you know you're going to run into multiple lineups similar to your own. The last thing you want is to have your kicker decide your fate. So bypassing a clear-cut value in favor of a lesser-utilized player might be sub-optimal to your average projected score, but optimal in terms of winning the tournament.

This is known as a "contrarian" strategy—one that differs from the consensus—and it has lots of value in large-field leagues.

Think about it like this. Assume you choose Lacy, who is 40 percent owned, and he has a huge day: 150 yards and two touchdowns. You have a large advantage over 60 percent of lineups, but you still need to compete with the other 40 percent, now with one less relevant position.

But if you select a much lesser-owned player—we'll say Chris Johnson who is just one percent owned in a given week— you'll have more positions at which you can gain an advantage over the field. So you're basically swapping a little value in hopes that you can make up for it with more "relevant" positions.

That's why it's often intelligent to start studs who appear to have poor matchups in tournaments. Players like Adrian Peterson and Calvin Johnson can have monster games against anyone, but when they go up against a stout defense, they often aren't heavily owned.

You can and should be a contrarian in those situations, targeting under-the-radar options who can ultimately increase your tournament win probability.

By the way, the data I showed you on GPP salary cap allocation is evidence that a contrarian strategy is of use in big leagues. Winning tournament teams spend $250 more on their defense than they do in 50/50s. Since most players try to save money on their defense, the extra few hundred bucks could go a long way in differentiating your lineup from others to help optimize your potential GPP win probability.

How to Play Tournaments on DraftKings

As I mentioned, I began playing heavily on DraftKings prior to even contacting them regarding this book. There are a bunch of reasons for that, one of which is their tournament structure.

Before you enter any league on any site, you should first check the payout structure. On DraftKings, you can simply click on the name of a league. If you do that, here's an example of what you'll see.

This GPP has a cap of 2,000 entrants. On the right side of the image, there's an area that lists the payouts. If you had taken down this particular league, you'd win $25,000 and an entry into DraftKings' Millionaire Grand Final.

If you could scroll down in that section, you'd see that the top 400 entrants are paid out—one-in-five. That's a much higher percentage than what you typically see elsewhere in the daily fantasy industry.

Since DraftKings pays out such a high percentage of entrants, you don't necessarily need to increase variance at all costs. You might still prefer to play a lineup with the greatest amount of upside possible, but a QB-WR-WR combination might be an option in this format since you can cash with a top 20 percent score.

Again, this GPP payout structure allows you all sorts of flexibility with how you structure your lineups. For the first time, large-field leagues can be an investment vehicle that's not so up-and-down. Instead of potentially entering dozens of leagues without cashing and ultimately compromising your bankroll, you can use lineup diversification to basically ensure cashing in DraftKings tourneys at a frequent rate.

The 10 Laws of Tournament Strategy

It doesn't matter if you're in a tournament, qualifier, multiplier, GPP, whatever—you need to approach it with a drastically different strategy from how you handle other league types. Here's a refresher of the important info from this chapter.

Law No. 1: Don't overlook the variance inherent to tournaments.

When you're deciding how much cash you can plunk down into any league, the most important question to ask yourself is "how often am I going to cash?" Even in tournaments with a flatter payout structure, you're an underdog to cash, regardless of your skills.

If you're entering tournaments as though you'll cash half of the time, you're probably going to regret it. Understand variance—accept that you're just going to get beat at times—

and you'll be able to better cope with losing and properly manage your money.

Law No. 2: Hedge against disaster by diversifying your tournament lineups.

Whereas using a single lineup or two is fine in head-to-head leagues, it's not a smart move in tournaments. By diversifying your lineups, you're trading in some of the upside that tournaments offer in exchange for a little safety.

Law No. 3: Draw from a larger pool of players.

I believe many daily fantasy players use an excessively small player pool in all league types, which stems from a failure to account for the fact that their projections could be wrong. Hopefully you can create accurate projections and values over time, but you can't make decisions as though your projections are always right.

If you have Josh Donaldson projected within a few percentage points of Mike Trout's value, does it really make sense to have massive exposure to Trout but none at all to Donaldson? No, and that's even truer in tournaments.

Law No. 4: Forget about traditional projections and values.

Projecting average points and creating values off of those projections is important in many league types, but traditional projections are useless in large-field leagues. You need upside, and that's all you need.

Law No. 5: Know when to pay for volatility.

One of the ways you can acquire a high ceiling is to pay for volatility, but you need to know when it makes sense. The data suggests paying for wide receivers and tight ends can be smart in tournaments because their points tend to come in bunches *and* they have the potential to really differentiate themselves from others at their position. In contrast, kickers are also volatile, but there's little deviation in their scores; without that scarcity, there's little reason to pay up for them.

Law No. 6: Always pair a quarterback with one of his receivers in a large GPP.

Pairing a quarterback with one of his receivers creates a dependent relationship that greatly enhances upside. You can also consider pairing your quarterback with two of his pass-catchers, but that's probably a better move in, say, a 50-man league (when you need upside but not necessarily a jaw-dropping ceiling) than it is in a huge GPP (when you absolutely must hit a home run).

Law No. 7: Stack your baseball tournament lineups in a big way.

Here's a little insider tip that I've uncovered while writing this book—a little something you won't find elsewhere: hitters on the same team face the same pitcher. You probably didn't know that, unless of course you have any conception at all of the sport of baseball.

It makes sense to stack teammates in tournaments because their production is tied to one another's, increasing upside. And although the daily fantasy world was a little unsure on the value of near full-team stacks versus stacking batters from two MLB teams, the evidence is in: you should load up on players on the same team in big tournaments. That's the best way to increase your upside.

And actually, the data supports small stacks in other league types, too. There's just not as much downside there as previously assumed. There are worse ways to approach a 50/50 than with two four-man stacks.

Law No. 8: Don't overlook pitching.

Pitchers are consistent from start to start, but they also have the potential scarcity that wins tournaments. In daily fantasy baseball, it makes sense to pay for their consistency and upside. That's especially true in small leagues, but it's possible in tournaments, too. If you have multiple stacks you're considering, go with the cheapest one that will allow you to secure the best pitchers (meaning the ones with the most consistency and highest ceilings).

Law No. 9: Go against the grain as a contrarian thinker.

You don't need to bypass every obvious value to go against the grain, but jumping on one or two players you know won't be highly owned can provide you with the lineup differentiation that you'll need in a tournament. One of the shrewd moves that I see again and again from the game's top pros is playing elite players in tough matchups; A.J. Green can get his numbers against any defense, but he won't necessarily be a popular choice against one of the league's top Ds.

The DraftKings tournament data also suggests it's smart to pay a few extra bucks for your defense in NFL tournaments. You'll separate yourself from the crowd, which typically goes cheap on their defense, and a huge day from your D of choice can provide a much-needed source of scarce points.

Law No. 10: Reduce tournament risk by playing them on DraftKings.

DraftKings kills the competition when it comes to tourneys because 1) they're running leagues with absolutely enormous amounts of cash and 2) they're paying out a much higher percentage of entrants than other sites.

When we talk about ROI, we really need to decipher between theoretical and practical. In theory, the payout structure doesn't necessarily matter over the long-run because we'll always see the same return over an infinite number of leagues.

But you know who doesn't have time to play an infinite number of leagues? Human beings who aren't immortal.

So what really matters is practical ROI—the amount of money you can realistically expect to return and how quickly you can turn it over to start the process anew—and DraftKings' tournament payout structure allows for an entirely unique approach to tournaments through which users don't need to wait weeks or months to cash in.

"The consequences of an act affect the probability of its occurring again."

- *B.F. Skinner*

5 The Final Piece of the Puzzle: Creating Projections and Lineups

"Most people ask what we would do if we had the answer. The first thing that we would do is we would begin to solve it. For example, picture a chess board and think about the rules that govern the game play. Just because you know how the pawns, bishops, and knights move around the board doesn't mean that you're a grand master."

- *Michio Kaku*

This book is set up in such a way that the majority of what you need to get started (and hopefully profit) playing daily fantasy football and baseball is located in the first four chapters. But as the great physicist Michio Kaku has pointed out, there's a difference between understanding all of the rules and truly mastering something.

Thus, this chapter is going to be filled with the opinions of daily fantasy's pros—the game's top players who are already highly profitable. Thanks to DraftKings, we know the rules of the game. Now it's time to hear from the grand masters.

Starting the Journey Toward Value

When it's all said and done, we're all seeking value; we want to uncover players whose production will exceed their cost. I've already explained how to build your research foundation, so how in the hell do we translate that data into player projections?

One way is to use the aggregate approach I detailed earlier. If you're creating daily fantasy football projections, for example, you can easily import data from numberFire, 4for4, FantasyPros, RotoGrinders, and similar sites into Excel.

By calculating the average of those projections, the hope is that you can factor out flaws in each set of projections to generate a "truer" mean projection. This "wisdom of the crowd" approach is the simplest and quickest way to create accurate projections.

But it's really only the start of your journey, because those projections must be modified as new information rolls in. The way that the projections are adjusted depends on the sport.

"Projecting baseball is a lot different than football because you're pretty limited with time in MLB," says CSURAM88. "So for baseball, I upload projections into Excel and then quickly modify them based on factors that aren't already part of the projections."

Another of daily fantasy baseball's best players—Mike5754— does the same. "After I have every player listed, I immediately delete anyone playing in a game that could rain out. If there's more than a 70 percent chance of rain, I won't start anyone in that game because it could kill my lineups if they don't play."

Talking with naapstermaan and other pros, there's a general consensus that studying the weather in baseball is vital to getting a sense of who's going to play and what they might do. "Even if there won't be rain during a game," says naapstermaan, "I might use heavy winds as a tiebreaker to target or fade hitters and pitchers based on the direction and speed of the wind."

For football, the pros seem to favor the Vegas lines more than the average player. Says CSURAM88, "Vegas is so accurate that it would be foolish to not consider their thoughts. I use Vegas as a foundation for my projections, so I'll usually bump up guys who are going to be in high-scoring games. Even if I don't change the projections all that much, it makes sense to target those players, especially when you can stack them in tournaments."

Mike5754 does the same in baseball. "I build around my pitchers. So I look at the Vegas lines to see who's projected to have a quality game, then I'll see what matches up with my initial projections. Then I'll consider other late news, like the weather, the opposition's batting order, the home plate umpire, and stuff like that."

Daily fantasy baseball players don't have time on their side, so the value of quick aggregate projections can be monumental. Daily fantasy football players have more time to study data (which ironically might be far less useful than the stats in baseball).

"Things change so much in the NFL that you really have to adjust on the fly," says CSURAM88. "The long-term numbers don't mean as much as they do in baseball because coaches get fired, schemes change, matchups mean a lot, and so on. So just slightly adjusting a player's past per-game averages doesn't work as well as it might in baseball."

Because of the time that can go into football projections and the fact that positions are so different from one another (as opposed to just batter vs. pitcher in baseball), let's quickly hit on the traits to seek at each position.

Building the NFL Prototype

There's lots of variance from week to week in the NFL, but ultimately, it's the same sorts of players who return value to daily fantasy owners. Their defining traits are the ones you want to emphasize in your projections.

Quarterback

I've already discussed mobility as a characteristic of high-floor signal-callers, but accounting for a high percentage of their team's touchdowns is also important.

CSURAM88 studies touchdown rates more than anyone. "Percentage of touchdowns is a really consistent stat for quarterbacks, so you always want to find players who are going to be major parts of their team's game plans.

Quarterbacks who see heavy workloads are obviously important, but you also want guys who throw the ball (or run it themselves) near the goal line. Peyton Manning has historically thrown the ball a lot inside the five-yard line, for example, and that's really important."

RotoGrinders is a great source for workload data, including important advanced red zone stats

.

Running Back

I've personally done a whole lot of research on running backs, so it's my most accurate position to project. Like quarterbacks, the workload matters a whole lot for backs. Check out the relationship between carries and year-end rank for backs over the past four seasons.

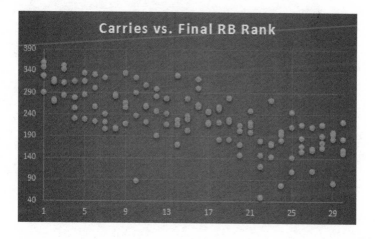

Pretty clear relationship—one that's much more linear than that for YPC and rank:

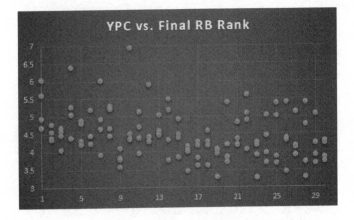

But everyone kind of knows that backs usually need to get the ball a lot to produce. What you might not have known is how much straight-line speed matters at the position. Check out the correlation for various pre-draft measurables and eventual NFL success for running backs. Note that the length of each bar matters most, not whether it's positive or negative.

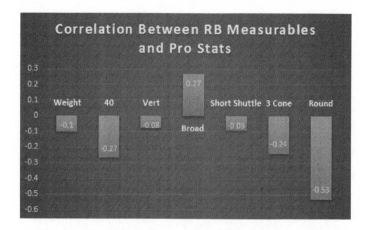

The most important trait, by far, is the round in which a back gets drafted. That doesn't mean NFL teams have efficiently drafted running backs, though; since 2000, those drafted in the mid and late rounds have actually recorded a higher YPC than those in the first two rounds. But early-round backs see heavy workloads, and that's what matters.

After that, though, you can see the two metrics that best capture explosiveness—the 40-yard dash and the broad jump—are most strongly correlated with running back success. And take a look at what happens if we break up the running backs into subcategories of 40 times.

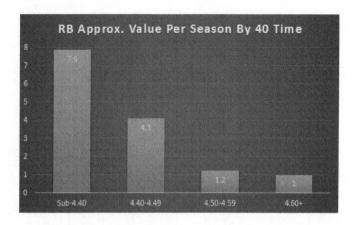

I used Pro Football Reference's approximate value—a metric that accounts for yards, touchdowns, receptions, and so on—to judge running backs. The numbers are revealing; if a running back doesn't run faster than a 4.50 at the NFL Scouting Combine, his odds of NFL success are miniscule.

These numbers are very applicable to daily fantasy football, too. First of all, you always want to have the most exposure to the types of players who find long-term success. It's not like season-long production comes completely independently of weekly production; the former is just the accumulation of the latter.

Second, stats like these can help to predict breakouts. When a rookie backup running back steps into the starting lineup for the first time, which happens all across the league every single season, it might be difficult to project him without a body of NFL work. His potential workload and his straight-line speed are the two most important factors in predicting his success, even on the level of a single game.

Wide Receiver/Tight End

At the wide receiver and tight end positions, I'm really interested in the same trait: size. Receivers who are big and heavy often find red zone success—a characteristic that's really consistent from year to year. Take a look at the red zone touchdown rates of DeSean Jackson (a horribly inefficient red zone receiver) and Dez Bryant (one of the game's premiere red zone receivers) since Bryant came into the NFL.

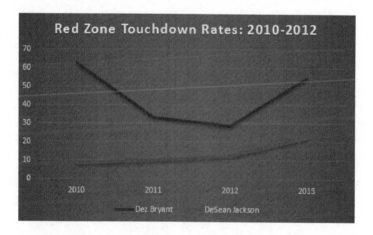

This difference is remarkable. And while I knew Bryant is efficient in the red zone, I actually had no idea what Jackson's numbers would be before I decided to use him as an example. I chose a small, big-play receiver who came to mind.

There's such an incredibly strong correlation between size and touchdowns for receivers that these numbers remain very consistent from year to year.

Overall, Bryant's career red zone touchdown rate is 41.7 percent and Jackson's is 12.8 percent. No matter how you slice it, touchdowns are incredibly important to daily fantasy owners. Even though they're relatively low-frequency, you still need to find a way to maximize their count in your lineups. It's a similar situation to targeting home runs in baseball; even though they're relatively fluky over the short-term, it's all about maximizing your exposure to the players who score touchdowns and hit home runs in an effort to increase your long-term win probability.

By the way, I personally find career red zone touchdown rates using PFR's Game Play Finder.

Building the MLB Prototype

As mentioned, baseball is very much a binary sport—it's always batter vs. pitcher with the conditions nearly exactly the same—so analyzing positions doesn't make as much sense as analyzing stats. Here's an overview of the most predictive baseball stats not used by the masses to help you adjust your initial aggregate projections. You can find all of them at FanGraphs.

Batting Average on Balls in Play (BABIP)

BABIP is one of my favorite stats in baseball because it can quickly give you an estimate of a hitter's luck in getting on base. For the most part, a player's BABIP is due to random factors, such as defensive strength, an exorbitant number of bloop hits, and so on. That means that BABIP typically regresses toward each player's career average (which is between .290 and .310 for most players).

When a player has been getting on base quite a bit when he shouldn't be, he'll have a higher-than-normal BABIP. When you see a BABIP in the .400 range over an extended period, it's a sign to steer clear of that hitter.

Weighted On-Base Average (wOBA)

wOBA is perhaps my favorite stat in all of baseball because it captures so many aspects of offensive play. In short, wOBA is a metric that accounts for the actual value of certain types of hits. Whereas batting average doesn't differentiate between the types of hits and on-base percentage inaccurately weighs the value of each type of hit, wOBA measures hits in proportion with their ability to create runs. That makes it a predictive stat.

One of daily fantasy baseball's top players—Mike5754—places serious emphasis on wOBA. "I look at wOBA more than any other stat. I'm always searching for guys with at least a 0.375 wOBA against either lefties or righties—whichever pitcher they're facing that day. So I immediately eliminate a bunch of players right out of the gate each day based on wOBA."

I spent some time charting wOBA for each position over the past few seasons. Here are the results.

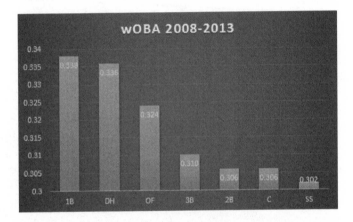

Unsurprisingly, first basemen and DHs have been the best hitters of the bunch. The average wOBA is around .320. It will be hard for anyone to sustain a wOBA in the 0.375 range on all at-bats over the long haul, but some can do it against just lefties or righties, especially over small sample sizes.

The point is that wOBA is highly predictive and an outstanding way to determine which hitters are likely to remain hot or break out of a slump in a given day.

Batter v L/R

One of the most popular ways to analyze matchups is with BvP (batter vs. pitcher) data, which you can find in a number of places around the Interwebs. However, there can be some big, big problems with BvP stats. Namely, they aren't big at all, i.e. a small sample size.

Even if a hitter has faced a particular pitcher, say, 100 times, his numbers will still be rather volatile. Over a stretch of 100 at-bats, he could hit .250 with two home runs, or he could hit .375 with 10 dingers. The at-bats might not be an incredibly small sample, but the other stats you want to study—hits, extra-base hits, homers, wOBA, whatever...that stuff is far flukier.

Mike5754 doesn't even look at BvP stats. "I just don't care because it can't be trusted. It's a small sample, but you also don't know the nature of the at-bats. Maybe a bunch came when the pitcher was throwing on short rest, for example. The only stats I consider when examining a batter versus a particular pitcher are those against lefties and righties. That's it."

And while some top daily fantasy players examine BvP in limited situations, most also tend to favor simple lefty/righty splits.

Batted Ball Data

It's really an amazing time to be a nerd. With the cumulative power of other geeks like me, we now have all sorts of data on not only the types of hits that pitchers allow, but also how their batted balls leave the bat (namely if they're ground balls, fly balls, or line drives).

That's important because it can give you a really strong indication of a pitcher's future success. The more ground balls, the better. The league average for ground balls is around 44 percent of all balls in play.

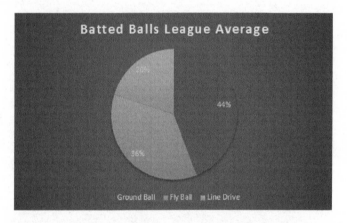

Stats like batting average allowed are flimsy, influenced heavily by BABIP, while batted ball rates show true pitcher quality. Historically, line drives have been worth 1.26 runs per out, fly balls worth 0.13 runs per out, and ground balls worth 0.05 runs per out, according to FanGraphs.

Even if you like a pitcher with a high ground ball rate, you might want to get away if he's also giving up line drives on more than 20 percent of batted balls. Since there are a huge number of runs created per out on line drives, minimizing it should be your top priority when analyzing pitchers.

Expected Fielding Independent Pitching (xFIP)

xFIP is another pitching stat that basically acts as an adjusted ERA, showing what a pitcher's ERA "should be," assuming 1) a league average BABIP and 2) a league average home run to fly ball rate (around 10 percent). Since we know both BABIP and home run to fly ball rate regress near a common league mean for pitchers, xFIP can sort out the noise to give us a really accurate idea of how pitchers are performing. It's an ERA you can trust.

Stats to Avoid: Batting Average, ERA, WHIP, Wins, BvP

Your typical daily fantasy player is going to look at some pretty generic stats to pick players: batting average, ERA, WHIP, wins, and maybe even batter vs. pitcher splits. None of those stats are nearly as predictive as those I listed, though. Batting average and WHIP, for example, don't control for changes in BABIP. All we really should care about is "can this stat help me make better projections?"

Ultimately, the reason that advanced stats, player prototypes, and the Vegas lines can be useful in your projections is because most players aren't considering that stuff in their work. The same is true of the daily fantasy sites that set the player salaries.

If you're creating initial projections based on aggregate data, you already have the basic predictors of success in there. If you try to adjust the numbers based on, say, recent touchdowns or ERA, your projections will just become repetitive. You need to search for important, predictive stats that *aren't already used by the masses* to obtain a true competitive advantage.

Projecting Players

The reason that I ran through some advanced stats is because I don't think there's necessarily one set way to project players. The process of doing research isn't just the means to an end; rather, it's often the most valuable piece of the puzzle. Analyzing objective values can help better inform your subjective decisions.

That's especially true in a sport like football that's not standardized in the same way as baseball. NFL teams run different schemes and approach the game as a whole differently from one another. That doesn't mean you should just guess on your player choices, though. Well, you *can* guess, but those guesses need to be calculated ones that are directed by your research.

One way that you can use advanced stats to help with your projections is to eliminate certain players right out of the gate. As mentioned, Mike5754 scans his favorite stat—Weighted On-Base Average—and considers only those players above a certain threshold over a given period of time. By choosing only those players who rank highly in a predictive advanced stat, you can greatly reduce the pool of players you need to project.

Salary Data and $/Point

If you're projecting players in Excel, you'll need to import salary data to create player values. You can typically download the salary data right from the daily fantasy sites, but you can also get it at RotoGrinders.

I want to quickly note that most daily fantasy players import salary data after projecting relevant players, but a few first look at the salaries. Mike5754 takes such an approach, importing MLB salaries into Excel, removing players he immediately deems overpriced (and then doing the same with Weighted On-Base Average) to generate a much more concentrated list of possible players.

Once you have a mean projection for each player (or the players you've chosen to project) and you've imported site salary data, you'll need to combine the two in order to create player values.

Most players create $/point values, simply dividing a player's salary by his projected points. If Jamaal Charles costs $9,000 and you have him projected to score 20.0 points, his $/point value would be $450. The lower the $/point, the better. All other things equal, you obviously want to pay as little as possible for each point that you can be expected to score.

Note that $/point values are especially relevant in head-to-head and 50/50 leagues, but not so much in tournaments. Remember, when you need upside, you really want to focus on obtaining players with high ceilings. The value matters and you still want to stick to primarily the top values in terms of $/point, but it's okay to work your way down your value list just a bit to make sure you acquire as high of a ceiling as possible.

Lineup Optimization

Some daily fantasy players use lineup optimization tools to figure out which lineup is "optimal" based on their projections. If you use Excel, "Solver" is a simple add-in that can help you optimize your lineup.

However, I find myself on the opposite end of the lineup creation spectrum, generally creating lineups by hand. The primary reason for that is that I don't believe Solver or other programs truly optimize your lineup since your projections aren't flawless.

Remember, projecting players (and $/point values) is a fragile process because little deviations in stats can throw off the results. Your projections can never perfectly capture a player's future from game to game, so there's lots of subjectivity in the lineup generation process.

Further, there are so many different players to project that you can create literally thousands of optimized lineups that are within a point or two of one another. That's a minute difference—one that's basically meaningless once you account for your fallibility as a prognosticator—so blindly choosing the true optimized lineup would be a mistake.

Use $/point values as a tool to find the lineup you consider to be the best for your goals in a particular league. With so many different lineup combinations, your aim should really be to put together a group of players who meet certain criteria (such as those related to the player prototypes and advanced stats).

Problems with $/Point

Before I dig into the problems with most value systems in even greater detail, let me preface this by saying that I think $/point has value (no pun intended) to daily fantasy players. It's a quick way to narrow down the list of potential players you can utilize in your lineups.

The main problem with $/point is the fragility on which I've already touched. The other chief issue is that it doesn't properly weight the importance of bulk points. That is, it's way more valuable for a high-priced (and thus highly projected) player to live up to his $/point than it is for a low-priced option to fulfill his $/point duties.

To show you why, I'm going to give you a very extreme and very awesome example. Suppose that the Dallas Cowboys sign me to play running back for their next game. Admittedly, this is very unlikely to happen (although many physicists would argue it necessarily must happen in some parallel universe somewhere).

So there I am, the starting tailback for the Cowboys, and DraftKings & Co. need to give me a salary. We'll just say for a second that DraftKings doesn't know I PLAYED HIGH SCHOOL FOOTBALL and that I still do 50 pushups (not in a row) every weekend. It's whatever.

Anyway, unaware of my natural ability, they price me at $0. Nothing. Zilch. Nada.

But you know I'm starting and you even project me for one yard. It might be one yard on 20 carries, but it's one yard. Guess what my value is with a $0 salary? It's $0/point, i.e. it's infinite. I have infinite value.

So while all those other sucker NFL players are sitting there with $/point values higher than $300, you can secure my one yard for a fraction of the cost, and that fraction is nothing.

But we all know that I'm not valuable at all. Putting me into your lineup would just be wasting a position; the $/point calculation has broken down. While situations obviously aren't so extreme in this universe, the idea is the same; lower-priced players will naturally have greater $/point values, but their actual worth to your team isn't represented by that number.

In short, you should be searching for the best combination of $/point and pure points.

Thinking in Probabilities

At the crux of this semi-negation of $/point as a flawless value system is that we should be thinking about players in a more probabilistic manner. To give you an idea of why, I'm going to jump right into an example.

Suppose you're deciding between a "high-low" running back combination of Adrian Peterson ($9,000) and Bernard Pierce ($5,000) versus a mid-tier combination of C.J. Spiller ($7,000) and Le'Veon Bell ($7,000). You have both duos projected to score 28.0 total points, so the $/point for both tandems is the same at $500.

Same projection, same total salary, same value. Even though they have identical $/point values, the second duo of Spiller and Bell is almost certainly the superior option. The reason is that the probability of both of them reaching a certain threshold of points is far greater than both Peterson and Pierce doing it (since Pierce's low probability kills their chances).

Let's assume that both Spiller and Bell have a 50 percent chance to score 14.0 fantasy points. The odds of both of them scoring at least 14.0 points would be 25 percent. Meanwhile, we'll say Pierce has a 30 percent chance to meet the mark.

So where would Peterson need to fall for he and Pierce to be the better running back pair? The answer is actually above 83 percent. Even if Peterson could be counted on to reach 14.0 points on four of five occasions, the chances of both he and Pierce doing it together would be only 24 percent.

And if we drop Pierce's probability just slightly to 25 percent—not unrealistic for a low-priced running back option who offers good $/point value—AP would need to score 14.0 points 100 percent of the time to make the Pierce/Peterson combo equal to the Spiller/Bell duo, and that obviously ain't happening.

Regardless of how you structure the numbers, the point is that players can have drastically different outlooks, even if they have the same $/point values, when you begin to assess them in terms of probabilities.

Points > Value

The reason that thinking probabilistically is valuable is because it places the emphasis back on projected points. Sometimes, daily fantasy players seem to get so caught up in value that they lose sight of the bigger picture: scoring a buttload of points.

Always remember that your goal isn't to maximize value at all costs. You could do that with a team of players who fill up only 60 percent of your cap. Instead, the ultimate goal is to maximize projected points (or the probability of your lineup reaching a certain threshold), and $/point or any other value system is just a tool to help you accomplish that.

Total Player Exposure

When you create your lineups, you'll need to decide how much you want to diversify. Some of the game's top pros don't do much lineup diversification at all.

CSURAM88 is one of them. "I play just one head-to-head lineup on each site. And even then, I'm using a lot of the same players across sites. But I don't put too much of my bankroll down on each one, so it's not really that risky."

For pros, diversifying lineups just means choosing sub-optimal players. Most will draw from a fairly large player pool in tournaments, but few play more than one (or at most, two) lineups in other leagues.

However, most pros don't have more than 20 percent of their total cash in play at any given time, and many fall below that mark. If you have a $100,000 bankroll, 20 percent is a whole lot of dough. If you have a $100 bankroll, not so much.

If you have limited funds and you want to put more than 20 bucks into play in a given night or weekend, though, you'll need to diversify just a bit more. What you should focus on most is the total exposure to each player.

In some cases, you need to be careful about using certain players together (a quarterback and his receiver in a heads-up league, for example, or two opposing running backs in a tournament). Otherwise, assuming the potential players you could place in your lineup aren't dependent on each other for production, the combination of players is less important than how often each individual is in your lineups.

If you're playing three DraftKings lineups and placing five percent of your bankroll into each one, the odds of you cashing depend on how the lineups differ from one another. If you don't have any of the same players, the leagues will basically be isolated events. If you use the same group of core players and switch around, say, a couple pitchers, the likelihood of winning or losing all three leagues will be much greater.

Thus, the lineups themselves matter less than the exposure to each player. Speaking with daily fantasy pros, it seems like most hover somewhere around the 10 percent mark for the ceiling on player exposure. That means if you're playing in three lineups with five percent of your bankroll in each one, you'd want to make sure no player is in more than two of those lineups. If you're putting only three percent down on each lineup, on the other hand, you can have your top guys in every lineup.

Hitting the Cap

If you sift through any daily fantasy sports forum or chat, you'll see that one of the most discussed topics is whether or not it's okay to leave cap space on the table. While there are a handful of players who trust their ability enough to go with their true optimal lineup and leave significant cap space out there, almost all of the pros at least come close to utilizing the entire cap.

In my opinion, you should almost always use the entire cap, for three reasons.

Fallibility

I must sound like such a pessimistic asshole by now. "You're going to be wrong. You're not as good as you think. Prepare for the worst." SHUT UP ALREADY.

No really though, once you start to account for your fallibility, you won't be so set on a particular lineup, increasing the value of filling up your cap.

Fragility

Remember, projections and player values are fragile— susceptible to big fluctuations via rather small changes in information. Because of that, it makes sense to hedge with the final reason to utilize all of your cap space...

Diversification

Since I advocate selecting from a player pool just slightly larger than your typical pro, it becomes easier to use all of your cap space. If you like a lineup that costs $59,000 out of a possible $60,000 on DraftKings, the number of viable options means you'll be able find somewhere useful to spend that extra $1,000.

All told, most pros usually come extremely close to using all of their cap space. "I tinker with my teams until I at least come close to filling the cap," Notorious told me. "I never leave more than one percent on the table. The only time that becomes an option is on a night in MLB when there isn't a full slate of games, and thus fewer players, or on a site that has weak pricing."

Walking You Through a Week of NFL

Because of the access I have to the game's top players, I thought it would be cool to walk you through their processes in both NFL and MLB. I spoke with four of the best daily fantasy players in the world—all ranked in the top 10 in at least one sport—to give you an idea of how they approach football and baseball.

CSURAM88's Approach to NFL

CSURAM88—Peter Jennings—is in this book quite a bit because, since working on my first daily fantasy book, we've become good friends. Peter is basically a full-time player at this point (how cool is that?), and I can say that he's hands-down the brightest NFL mind I've met.

We talk each week about upcoming values, and the amount of time he spends on research is always apparent. I really couldn't recommend a better player to teach anyone about daily fantasy football (or basketball—his favorite sport). Let's let him walk you through his NFL process.

"I start by looking at each site's salaries on Tuesday just to get a sense of who might be valuable. Sometimes people get so involved with the numbers that they don't even think about who just pops out as an obvious value.

Throughout the week, I watch a lot of film. That's important in the NFL because the stats aren't necessarily standardized in the same way as other sports. And there might be different aspects of each contest—the game flow or just how a player looks—that you can't see in the box score.

There's a lot that can go into my projections, but I really take advantage of the Vegas lines. They're so helpful and if I'm bullish on a player in a game that Vegas thinks will be high-scoring, that's just more confirmation that he's probably a great value.

One of the ways I use the lines is to project player touchdowns. Let's say the Broncos are projected to score X points. I can look at their past scoring distribution to get an idea of how many touchdowns that will be. Then I start to distribute those scores to players based on their past likelihood of scoring.

So if the Broncos are projected to score four touchdowns and I know that Peyton Manning accounts for 75 percent of Denver's touchdowns, then my projection for him will be right around three touchdowns. Even though the total touchdowns can change versus different opponents, a player's "market share" of touchdowns on his own team tends to remain the same over time.

I also use Vegas player props to get a sense of projected yards, but I'll tweak those based on different information we learn throughout the week. I look at stats on Football Outsiders, Pro Football Focus, and RotoGrinders.

I specifically look at target data for receivers and snap data for all players, especially running backs. Running backs need lots of carries to give you value, so the snaps are important. When a running back is seeing a lot of snaps and is playing on a team that Vegas projects to win easily, he'll probably have a heavy workload. Red zone and goal line snaps are really important, too. I target players who get the ball near the goal line because they usually account for a high percentage of their team's touchdowns.

In addition to snaps, I also care about players' "percentage of workload stats," which are at RotoGrinders. So not only how often is he on the field, but how frequently does he see the ball when he's playing? What percentage of his team's touches, yards, and touchdowns does he account for?

Another stat I examine is how each defense performs versus particular positions. I think that's a step or two ahead of most players. If a novice is projecting a No. 1 wide receiver, for example, he might look at how many yards the defense has allowed. A little bit better player might look at how the defense performs against only wide receivers. But I'd look at how that defense performs solely against the other team's top receiver. Maybe they're poor against the pass overall but have one really good cornerback who shuts down No. 1 receivers.

I also use Pro Football Focus for a lot of that data because they have individual defensive player stats. So if I see news that a particular cornerback will shadow a receiver or a linebacker will play most snaps against a pass-catching running back, I can examine their coverage stats to see if it's smart to target or fade the offensive player.

There are so many injuries and personnel changes in football each week that value can shift really quickly. If a backup running back is thrust into the starting lineup, for example, that's obviously going to drastically change his projection. But even small news, like a coach saying he's going to get a wide receiver more targets, can be useful. So I just stay updated with player news throughout the week and alter my projections accordingly.

I use Excel Solver to give me optimal lineups based on my projections, but I don't just pick the top one no matter what. There's all sorts of considerations that go into the lineup, like the player combinations, their upside and risk, and the league type.

I make one optimal lineup for head-to-head games on each site, and I start to enter those on Saturday. I usually stay up all night submitting lineups and don't stop until right before kickoff on Sunday. So I'm pretty tired by the time the game's start. But you have to monitor your players, obviously, in case a questionable player is a late scratch or something.

Also, I usually do heads-up lineups first and then tournament lineups later because it gives me extra time to see where there might be overlay in some tournaments. When there's lots of overlay, I'll usually enter a lot of lineups because that's clearly a +EV situation for me."

And there you have it.

Headchopper's Approach to NFL

In Week 9 of the 2013 season, a man who goes by the name of headchopper turned in what many consider to be the greatest week in the history of daily fantasy football. Winning tickets to all of the industry's major qualifiers, headchopper took down the DraftKings Sunday 200 Grand (for a $25,000 grand prize) and won a ridiculous 25 tickets into the Millionaire Grand Final. You could buy into that tournament for $1,500, meaning the value of those tickets was just under $40,000. Not a bad weekend.

Headchopper posted nearly 300 points on DraftKings that week (yes, 300 points in the NFL), which is outrageous. It wasn't just a lucky week, though, because headchopper is consistently near the top of the GPP leaderboards. At the time of this writing, he's the sixth-ranked tournament player in the world.

I spoke with the man, the myth, the legend about his NFL strategy.

"My approach to daily fantasy football is a little bit different than most because I don't put as much stock in all of the projections. I think it's more valuable to spend time researching players, looking at matchups, and reading analysis throughout the week.

The first thing I do each week is look at the player salaries. From there, I can create an initial player pool of guys I like or would potentially use. That changes each week, but it's usually around 12 quarterbacks, 18 running backs, 24 receivers, and 12 tight ends.

Then I cut down that list based on matchups, injuries, and stuff like that. I look around the internet at all sorts of analysis and I study others' rankings. I don't use anyone else's rankings in isolation, but if a lot of guys I respect are high on someone, then I'll take a closer look at him too.

Once I have a smaller player pool, I can start making lineups on Saturday. I usually enter cheap tournaments—like $1 and $2—as a way to practice making lineups. I just mess around with different player combinations and just try to figure out what I like. I'll usually fall in love with a couple of those, so those are the lineups I enter into larger tournaments.

A lot of daily fantasy players use lineup optimizers and other tools like that, but I think there's so much subjectivity in it that I'm better off just making lineups on my own by hand and figuring out what works. I play a lot of tournaments, so I'm always looking for upside. I don't necessarily force stacks, though; it just depends on the situation. For example, some quarterbacks are really likely to throw to their No. 1 receiver—Matthew Stafford to Calvin Johnson, for example—so they pair better together than a quarterback who spreads the ball around more.

Another thing that I don't do is intentionally fade high-value players. I know some people like to do that in big tournaments to create a unique lineup, but if a guy is a great value, I'll play him. I also don't play guys who aren't great values just to force them into my lineups. I just go with who I like.

I usually have a handful of players I'll target, and I use them pretty much everywhere. So in Week 9 when I scored all those points, I really liked Andre Johnson and T.Y. Hilton. I put them in pretty much every lineup and then diversified around them. Sometimes I like even more guys as my core and I'll just mix and match my other values around those guys. So I don't necessarily hedge as much as the average player because I want to stick to the core group of optimal values.

On DraftKings, I place a lot of emphasis on receivers. I usually pay for receivers pretty heavily since it's full PPR and you can also use one in the flex. I almost always have a wide receiver in the flex in that format."

Walking You Through a Day of MLB

To walk you through a typical day of projections and lineup creation for daily fantasy baseball, I spoke with one of the game's premiere cash players (Mike5754) and the current No. 1 ranked tournament player in the world (naapstermaan) to give you two different perspectives.

Mike5754's Approach to MLB

Sticking primarily with head-to-heads and 50/50s, Mike5754's MLB strategy is about risk-minimization.

"After I download salary data from the sites and eliminate players I recognize as immediately overvalued, I look at the Vegas lines to see which pitchers are projected to do well. I always build my lineups around my pitchers, no matter the league, because they should be your source of consistent points. That usually means paying up for the more expensive ones.

One thing I do differently than a lot of players is pick hitters by targeting poor pitchers. I use the lines to see which pitchers are struggling, and then select from a group of potential batters who are facing those pitchers. I think the pitcher is so important and so consistent that it's really valuable to study pitcher stats for batters.

I also look at past stats for hitters, of course. I don't consider BvP stats much because they're usually fluky and small samples, but I do really care about batter vs. lefty/righty. Since I play mostly head-to-heads, I typically prefer batters with balanced stats versus lefties and righties. The reason for that is because starting pitchers can come out of the game pretty quickly sometimes, so you want hitters who can hit well against anyone. That raises their floor, which is obviously important in heads-up games.

If you pick a player who hits extraordinarily against righties but horrible against lefties, he could be in trouble if he starts slow and the opponent brings in a lefty within the first few innings. I'm more likely to target hitters with unbalanced lefty/righty splits in tournaments when I want upside. Otherwise, I'd prefer a hitter who hits .290 against both lefties and righties over someone who hits .310 against lefties but .200 against righties, even if they're both facing a lefty starter.

I also favor long-term stats more than recent play. I think hitters can get hot and cold in MLB, but for the most part, I prefer to play the law of averages. So I'd say I build projections based on long-term data and then adjust for recent play.

I don't necessarily mind small stacks in head-to-head leagues. Since I'm targeting batters against a handful of struggling pitchers, it usually ends up happening anyway. You just need to trust your research. If I'm playing teammates, though, I prefer to pick guys hitting near one another in the order because you can increase your upside with RBI situations, but it's not really risky.

After I've done projections, I'll create one or two optimal lineups for the night. I hedge a little bit just to limit my downside, but not too much because I want to stick to the top values. I also have very strict bankroll management, so that allows me to use just a single lineup if I'd like because I'm not going overboard with entries. I usually put around five percent of my bankroll into play in a given night in MLB, and never more than 10 percent.

I also enter more 50/50 leagues than I do in football. The reason is that with the consistency of pitchers, I think you can guarantee a pretty high floor, which you can't do as easily in football. So that makes my MLB lineups naturally better-suited for leagues in which a high floor is valuable."

Naapstermaan's Approach to MLB

Naapstermaan is widely considered the top tournament player in the world. As of the time of this writing, here's a list of his biggest cashes.

Biggest Scores					
Site	Sport	Date	Game Type	Rank	Points
🦅	⚾	Jul 21st	$200.00 Salary	1 / 2373	2545.64
🦅	⚫	Mar 29th	$200.00 Salary	1 / 825	1350.49
◇	⚾	Aug 24th	$10000.00 Salary	6 / 40	784.05
🦅	⚾	Jun 16th	$100.00 Salary	2 / 1014	665.28
🦅	⚾	Apr 14th	$200.00 Draft	3 / 722	644.86
◇	⚾	Aug 24th	$10000.00 Salary	9 / 40	614.74
🦅	⚾	Jul 21st	$200.00 Salary	13 / 2373	546.3
🦅	⚫	Mar 29th	$200.00 Salary	6 / 825	460.89

The dollar amounts are just the buy-ins, so you can see how profitable he's been in his career. He won the largest single payout in daily fantasy baseball history--$125,000 in DraftKings' Midsummer Classic baseball championship. There's no better person to break down tournament strategy than naapstermaan.

"I start all of my baseball research by checking the weather. If it looks like it might rain in a game, I'll fade those players. I'll also fade hitters in stadiums with heavy wind blowing in or pitchers with heavy wind blowing out. So I immediately eliminate certain guys right off the bat.

Then I look at the Vegas lines, which gives me an idea of which pitchers to target. Because I play mainly tournaments, I use a pretty diverse group of players. I roll out different stacks and then fill in the pitchers based on the remaining salary cap. I do the opposite when I play heads-up, but I think pairing the right groups of hitters is important in tournaments so you can create synergy and increase upside.

The exact stacks I use are based on the payout structure. In qualifiers that pay out just the top entrant or other tournaments that have a top-heavy payout structure, I use a one-team stack. I think that gives me the most possible upside (Note from Jonathan: That fits with the DraftKings data). If it's a flatter payout structure, I might use a two-team stack because I don't necessarily need unlimited upside and it can help me cash it a little more often.

Same idea with the size of the tournament. In smaller tourneys, I might be more inclined to use a two-team stack than in a huge GPP that requires a massive ceiling.

In terms of stats, I actually look at BvP stats quite a bit, but not because I care that much about them for my own projections. I look at them because I know a lot of other players are doing the same, so it helps me figure out who might be really popular in a given night. If I'm deciding between two stacks and one has some hitters with quality stats versus that night's starting pitcher, I'd be more likely to fade that team so that I can have a unique lineup. That's a little contrarian strategy that's useful in tournaments.

I also like hitters who hit early in the order because they're obviously more likely to get more at-bats and more points. When I try to save money on a player who is really cheap, I almost always try to make sure he hits in one of the top four spots in the order.

I still think there's a lot of subjectivity that goes into daily fantasy, even in baseball, so the most helpful tactic for me is discussing potential plays with other good players. I like to chat with other pros throughout the day to get a sense of who they like and we can bounce ideas off of each other. So for anyone who is new to daily fantasy, I think finding experienced players you can trust and then picking their brains is the best thing you can do."

Playing NFL on DraftKings

If you're playing daily fantasy sports, the general principles remain the same no matter where you play. But it's important to keep in mind that the implementation of those philosophies should change based on the site on which you're playing.

There are a few differences between daily fantasy sites, the most obvious of which are deviations in scoring and starting lineup requirements. So I want to give you an idea of what you should be examining when approaching either daily fantasy football or baseball at a particular site. And since we have all of this data from DraftKings at our disposal, they're the obvious choice to analyze.

So here are some of the subtle nuances of DraftKings' scoring and lineup requirements that mastering can turn a good player into a great one.

PPR

DraftKings rewards a full point per reception, which changes the value of some positions relative to one another. The most obvious effect is that wide receivers and tight ends hold more value. PPR scoring increases the scarcity of the top receivers; it creates another category through which they can differentiate themselves.

It also decreases the importance of quarterbacks. Passers are already of limited value on DraftKings because they receive only four points per passing touchdown and one point per 25 yards. There's not as much scarcity at the position as if the quarterbacks got six points per score and one point per 20 yards, so it can be advantageous to go a little lower at the position, especially in tournaments when you don't need consistency. That also fits with the data, which shows that winning GPP lineups spend $350 less at quarterback than winning 50/50s.

Bonuses

DraftKings gives you three points for 300 passing yards, 100 rushing yards, or 100 receiving yards. I think one of the areas daily fantasy players can go wrong is trying to predict bonus points. On the individual level, they're volatile enough to just ignore them. Sure, Drew Brees is more likely than a rookie quarterback to reach 300 yards, but that effect is the same across positions.

On the positional level, though, the bonuses mean something. If you're trying to figure out how to efficiently allocate cap space among positions, it's obviously valuable to know which ones are the most important. So I charted the occurrences of the bonuses from 2008 to 2012.

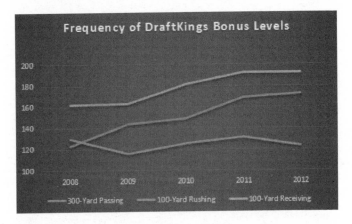

You can see that 100-yard receiving performances have been the most common in every season. Part of that is probably due to a larger potential player pool since teams could theoretically have three receivers go for 100 yards in a game, whereas typically just one running back has a shot to crack that barrier.

However, the difference in 100-yard games is large enough to suggest it's at least as likely that your receiver will go for 100 yards as your running back. Second, quarterback and wide receiver bonuses are increasing, whereas running back bonuses have remained steady, suggesting that quarterbacks and pass-catchers are becomingly increasingly more important in relation to running backs.

Again, bonuses are relatively fluky, so it's not like they should be an enormous factor in your projections; you should still consider paying for running backs in head-to-head leagues, for example, since they're more consistent than wide receivers on a weekly basis.

The main aspect of lineup creation in which bonus points are meaningful is the flex...

The Flex

If you're searching for the biggest possible advantage you can uncover in the world of DraftKings daily fantasy football, you just found it. The flex spot allows you the opportunity to gain a major advantage over other players because most approach it inefficiently.

When I discussed the flex position with the top daily fantasy players, the majority said they almost always play a wide receiver in the flex in PPR leagues. On a $/point basis, wide receivers consistently offer the most value on DraftKings. Now, that's always subject to change if the site alters the way they price their players (so do your research), but it's unlikely to vary too much since pass-catchers naturally offer more value in PPR leagues.

So when I got this data from DraftKings on the win rates for head-to-head lineups with different positions in the flex, I was a little surprised.

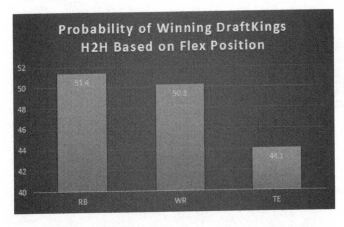

I say "a little surprised" because you have to remember that running backs offer far more safety than wide receivers and tight ends. If you can find cheap running backs expected to see a surge in workload, it should be a fairly consistent source of points.

Further, my hunch is that most players have been using receivers pretty much interchangeably. By targeting solely slot receivers who have proven to be more consistent, the wide receiver-in-the-flex lineups might win a little more frequently.

The real surprise here comes at tight end, as only 44.1 percent of lineups that used a tight end in the flex won their head-to-head matchups. With 10,300 total leagues in this data set, the results are stunning and undeniably significant. Since tight ends usually don't offer value comparable to that of receivers in terms of $/point *and* their week-to-week production is relatively volatile, it seems like you should avoid them as flex plays except in really extreme situations.

Meanwhile, this is evidence that running backs are indeed in play as head-to-head (and 50/50) flex options. They're predictable, and there's value in that. You can and should still consider wide receivers, too, especially those who see shorter targets from the slot.

Also note that this is perhaps substantial evidence that we need to concern ourselves with more than $/point calculations. The reason is that daily fantasy players are unanimous in agreement that running backs offer the worst $/point values on DraftKings. Yet due to their consistency, they make perhaps the best head-to-head flex options. When you begin to view players in terms of probabilities, traditional conceptions of value get turned upside-down.

In addition to head-to-head leagues, I also have data on how different flex strategies affect GPP success.

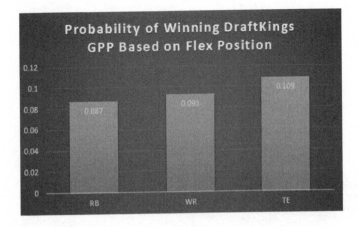

Again, this is shocking—the reverse of what we see in head-to-head leagues. These results suggest it is indeed smart to pay for volatility in large leagues that require upside. Yes, running backs are a more consistent source of points, but they might not have the same sort of home run ability as wide receivers (or even tight ends, relative to their salaries) in PPR leagues.

I wouldn't just go throwing tight ends in the flex, however. The reason is that the numbers are distorted due to the success of the NFL's elite tight ends (namely Jimmy Graham and Rob Gronkowski). How do I know that? This...

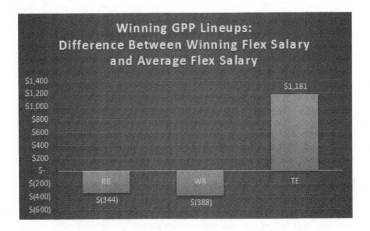

The average salary of a flex tight end in a GPP lineup was $5,329. The average salary of a flex tight end in a GPP lineup *that won*, however, was $6,420. That's a huge jump and one that we don't see at the other positions. Actually, winning GPP lineups typically spend less on the flex at positions other than tight end—a position that truly seems distorted because of a couple outliers.

Thus, unless you're going to use an elite tight end in both the tight end slot and the flex position, it's probably smartest to stick with wide receivers as GPP flex plays on DraftKings.

Playing MLB on DraftKings

Your approach to daily fantasy baseball can be even more site-specific than daily fantasy football since MLB scoring can vary so much. To give you an idea of how DraftKings' MLB scoring compares to that on other daily sites, I charted the difference between DraftKings and the aggregate of the other major sites as a function of points for a home run.

On DraftKings, for example, a home run is 10 points and a triple is eight (80 percent). Comparing values in this way allows us to gauge the relative importance of each stat in a more accurate way.

Batter Scoring

Check out the relative importance of offensive statistics on DraftKings.

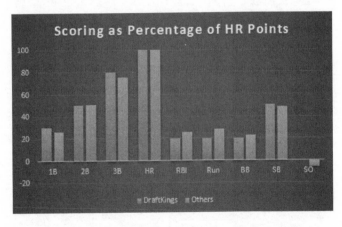

There aren't any major deviations here. DraftKings values singles, triples, and stolen bases just slightly more than the typical site, where they reward fewer points for RBIs, runs, and walks.

Note that hitters cannot go negative on DraftKings because they don't lose points for strikeouts. That's important because it increases the worth of batters who hit early in the order. Those players have a little extra value on DraftKings since every at-bat has a positive expectation; nothing negative can result from more plate appearances. Some daily fantasy pros like to stack the 1-2-3-4 hitters from two teams, for example.

The fact that you don't lose points for strikeouts means you can also do what the consistency stats from the previous chapters suggest is correct: pay for home runs. A lot of power hitters also strike out more than normal, but that won't hurt you on DraftKings. You'll need to balance between hitters early in the lineup and later guys since it's typically the 3-4-5-6 batters with the most power, but when you come across, say, a player who hits from the 2 spot and he's a home run guy, that's really valuable.

Pitcher Scoring
I also charted pitcher scoring as a function of points for a win.

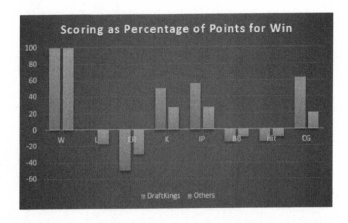

DraftKings doesn't take away points for a loss, but you lose more points for earned runs, walks, and hits. However, the high value of strikeouts and innings pitched more than compensates for the potential negative points. The site also weighs complete games a lot, although those are pretty rare.

Nonetheless, your goal on DraftKings should be searching for strikeout pitchers who typically go deep in games. To give you an idea of the value of a strikeout on DraftKings, consider that two of them equate to an entire win. That means you don't need to worry all that much about if your pitcher is on a great team that's expected to win the game; a guy who gives you eight innings and allows two runs in a loss is still plenty valuable.

Two pitchers
You must start two pitchers on DraftKings, which of course increases their importance. The site's scoring increases the

potential variance at the position; poor pitchers can have really bad games, and elite ones can give you something special. The matchups matter, but in almost every scenario, you want to pay for the consistency of top-tier pitchers *at both starting spots*.

The Late Lineup Switch

As mentioned, DraftKings is unique in allowing late lineup switches, i.e. you can substitute out any player for another any time prior to their games starting. That's valuable for NFL leagues that start on Thursday night, but also for MLB weekend games.

On the weekend, the games are typically spread out throughout the day. On most sites, your lineup is locked once the first game begins. But what if there's a late scratch or a pitcher change? Well, you're screwed. Not so on DraftKings, where you can edit your lineup to ensure you never start someone who isn't playing.

The 10 Laws of Projections and Lineups

Peter Jennings once told me "If you can create accurate projections, you can be a profitably daily fantasy player. If you can't, you won't." Here are the take-home points on making projections and constructing lineups.

Law No. 1: Use Vegas as a foundation.

They say what happens in Vegas, stays in Vegas. But if you're
a daily fantasy player and what happens in Vegas stays there,
you're leaving money on the table. This was a law from a
previous chapter, too, because it's so important.

The Vegas lines are especially useful in NFL tournaments,
when you're favoring massive upside, and in all types of
baseball leagues. Because there's not a whole lot of time to
perform in-depth projections on every MLB player since they
play daily, many pros use the Vegas lines to target strong
pitchers in low-scoring games and teams hitting against weak
pitchers.

Law No. 2: Import salary data.

At least one of daily fantasy baseball's premiere players—
Mike5754—imports salary data to immediately eliminate
players he recognizes as overvalued. That cuts down on the
pool of players he needs to analyze, thus reducing research
time.

Either way, you'll need to import salary data to create values
for each player. A $/point calculation is the most popular for
most players—how many dollars you must spend per point
you can be expected to score. While $/point shouldn't be
used as a standalone tool in creating lineups, it's still
important to identify the best values.

Law No. 3: Think about which types of NFL players will help you reach your goals.

In football, there are specific player types that continually perform the best—fast running backs with heavy workloads and big, red zone-relevant receivers, for example. If you want consistency, consider mobile quarterbacks, pass-catching running backs, and slot receivers. If you want a higher ceiling, emphasize speed at the running back position and a heavy workload, especially in the red zone, for all positions.

Law No. 4: Consider which stats are most important for MLB players.

Since baseball is a binary sport, the positions matter less than they do in football. A "prototypical" second baseman, for the purposes of daily fantasy, is the same as a "prototypical" shortstop.

The most consistent stats are home runs and strikeouts. That means you should generally load up on power hitters, typically in the 3-4-5 spots, and pitchers with a lot of Ks. Because of the deviation in those stats, you should favor them in all league types.

Law No. 5: Think about players in terms of probabilities.

Strict $/point calculations are important, but they also overvalue low-salary players. There's value in, well, value, but there's also value in pure points. When Jamaal Charles matches his projection, that's more valuable to you than if a running back who costs half as much does the same.

In addition to $/point, consider how likely each player might be to match certain thresholds. One player projected to score 20 points might have a significantly wider distribution of possible outcomes than another player projected at the same mean score. Because you should be targeting different sorts of players in different leagues, a probabilistic manner of thinking is just as valuable—perhaps more so—than the deterministic approach that stems from traditional value calculations.

Law No. 6: Don't leave more than one percent (and preferably less) of your cap space.

The main reason failing to utilize cap space is a problem is that it assumes your projections are flawless. Again, if you're thinking in terms of probabilities, you'll realize you're going to be wrong at times. Once you account for your imperfections, the pool of potential players you're willing to utilize increases, thus making it highly unlikely that the true "optimal" lineup doesn't come close to maxing out the salary cap.

Law No. 7: Monitor the weather, especially in baseball.

Wind can wreak havoc on passing games in the NFL, but
football games almost never get cancelled. Meanwhile,
baseball games get rained out all the time. Starting a player
or two in a game that rains out can be disastrous. Further,
you should monitor wind speeds to help you select batters
and pitchers.

Law No. 8: Utilize late-game swap when possible.

The primary advantage that a late-game swap feature offers
is that it allows you to play your true best lineup right out of
the gate, regardless of when leagues begin. If you're in an NFL
league that starts on Thursday night, for example, you can
use a player who is questionable for a Sunday game, knowing
that if he doesn't go, you aren't in major trouble. When that
feature is taken away, it decreases the aggressiveness with
which you can approach early lineup choices.

Law No. 9: Understand site scoring and lineup requirements.

It's absolutely critical to understand site scoring and lineup
requirements. There's a massive difference between
standard scoring and PPR scoring in the NFL, for example, and
failing to account for that could ruin your chances for success.

For football, DraftKings is a full PPR site that gives bonuses for 100-yard rushing/receiving games and 300-yard passing games, so that benefits wide receivers. Since DraftKings requires you to start someone in the flex, it really increases the importance of wide receivers.

For baseball, DraftKings has no negative points for hitters, increasing the value of those hitting at the top of the order who will see the most plate appearances. Pitcher scoring is volatile, but it increases the deviation between elite and low-end guys. In almost every case, you should be play a high-priced pitcher in both starting spots.

Law No. 10: Don't overlook subjective factors.

Although most daily fantasy players project players, the best ones don't let the numbers control their actions. There are all sorts of subjective factors that should influence your decisions, so don't feel like you need to follow the data 100 percent of the time.

The main reason for that is because the process of researching, doing projections, and creating lineups is valuable in and of itself. If you approach daily fantasy with the sort of "I have a lot to learn" mentality that makes the greatest players as good as they are, your subjective thoughts will be influenced by objective factors anyway, so it's okay to "trust your gut" when that's the case.

(Bonus) Law No. 11: Consider running backs in the flex in heads-up leagues, but not in tournaments.

I think the flex data from DraftKings is so interesting that I gave it its own bonus law. It's particularly noteworthy that running backs, despite generally poor $/point value relative to the other positions, make for the best flex plays because of their predictability.

In large GPPs, though, you should typically fade running backs as flex plays and target either a big-play wide receiver or an elite tight end—both of whom can be excellent sources of scarce upside.

"The creation of a thousand forests is in one acorn."

- *Ralph Waldo Emerson*

6 Getting Analytical: An Appendix of Extra Data

"It is a critical mistake to theorize before one has data."

- *Arthur Conan Doyle*

This book has obviously been extremely analytical, so my sincerest apologies go out to those of you who thought you were getting a vague, subjective book that would propose no actionable advice (but I assure you there are plenty of those on the market for you). So here we are, stuck with all these numbers that can help us make lots of money.

Seriously though, I hope I've been able to break down the math and data in such a way that it makes sense. Einstein (I think it was Albert, but it might have been his little-known brother, Jimmy) once said "if you can't explain it to a six-year old, you don't understand it," and I find that to be true in many ways. The data itself might get complex at times, but the bottom line should be simple.

I've spent the last few years performing all sorts of fantasy sports-related analyses in an effort to become a better player. When combined with all of the incredible data provided to me by DraftKings, I'm sitting on countless Excel spreadsheets that I feel hold information that could lead to actionable advice for daily fantasy players. I collected all of the data on prototypical NFL players from the last chapter, for example, and it's shaped the way I approached daily fantasy football.

So this chapter will be a collection of just a few pieces of data for which I couldn't necessarily find a spot in the main portion of the book. If any of it helps you become a better daily fantasy player, that's great, and if not, well, uh, just pretend I didn't even write it.

Note that you won't find "The 10 Laws" at the end of this appendix. Those sections were meant to provide "bottom line" analysis, but I hope to interpret each piece of data and provide meaningful advice within the text of this chapter.

Pitching vs. Hitting

For much of this book, I've talked about the importance of paying for pitchers. Here's a little more evidence that's the way to go.

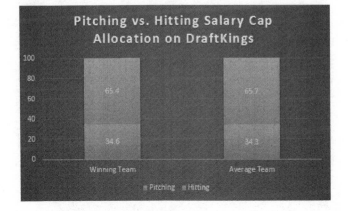

The typical DraftKings winning lineup has spent 0.3 percent more on pitching than the average team. Again, with the thousands and thousands of lineups analyzed, that's a significant number. It's sort of like the difference between a 4.39 40-yard dash and a 4.49 40-yard dash or the difference between mercury levels of 0.30 parts per million and 0.50 parts per million in your fish—small differences, large effect.

*Note: I quickly Googled that mercury thing and I have no idea if that really constitutes a big difference in mercury, but the first site I visited suggested that's the case, sooooooo, yeah.

NFL Defensive Strength

A little while back, I did some research on defensive strength from season to season, analyzing how specific defensive ranks (such as run defense) carried over from year to year.

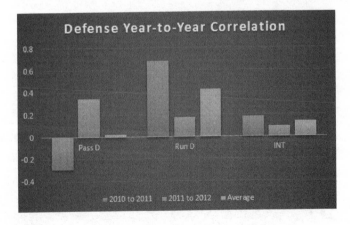

There seemed to be no correlation between pass defense from one year to the next, a moderate correlation for team interceptions, and a strong correlation for run defense.

To test that further, I looked back at the strength of the run defense correlation over a five-year sample.

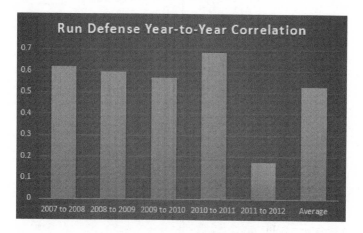

While pass defense is relatively fluky from season to season, run defense remains very consistent. But why?

I think the answer is that run defense more accurately reflects actual team strength. The best teams are typically winning late in games, so their final run defense rank is usually pretty high since they don't see as many attempts. It's just the opposite for the worst teams, who see a lot of rushes late in games.

You might say that we should see the same sort of effect with pass defense; if the best teams are winning and get thrown on a lot, they should give up more yards. That's true to an extent, but it's also important to remember that pass defense is more vital to team success than run defense. Many times, teams acquire leads by throwing the ball effectively and stopping the pass, then milk it away with the run. So the winning teams that get passed on a lot late in games probably didn't give up many passing yards earlier, meaning they wouldn't rank as low overall, despite the extra attempts.

I think this data has obvious uses early in the season. Namely, we don't necessarily need to be too concerned about team pass defense early in the year; chances are it won't resemble what we saw in the prior season. The opposite is true for run defense.

However, there's another important point here; perhaps we should care more about the opponent for running backs than any other position. Remember, early passing success typically creates a lead, which results in fewer passing attempts late in the game. That means the numbers for quarterbacks, wide receivers, and tight ends might "even out" a bit as games progress; if they're efficient early, they'll get their numbers then. If they're not, they'll probably be down in the game and make up for it with more attempts late.

The same effect doesn't exist for running backs; most of them are more dependent on game situations for touches. When you consider the consistency of run defense, it means we might want to place more weight on favorable matchups for backs than other positions. The easiest way to do that is to search for running backs with projected heavy workloads on teams that are the favorites to win the game.

Best Player Owned Frequency

One of the strategies proposed in the chapter on tournament play is using a contrarian approach—purposely going against the grain in order to create a unique lineup. Up until now, it was just assumed that bypassing a few "obvious" values was optimal in tournaments. Now, the evidence is in.

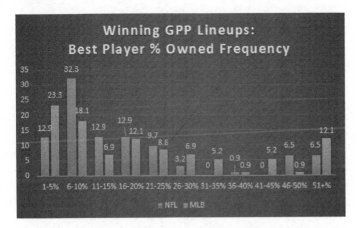

This graph shows the percentage of winning GPP lineups with top-scoring players in specific usage brackets (represented with the percentages at the bottom). For example, the two bars all the way to the left show the percentage of winning GPP lineups in both NFL (12.9 percent) and MLB (23.3 percent) with a high-scoring player who was owned on anywhere between one and five percent of all lineups.

The data on this graph is extremely interesting and should make us think about how we structure our tournament lineups. Namely, look at how important it is to have a low-usage player who erupts for a huge game. Of all winning GPP lineups, 45.2 percent of daily fantasy football teams and 41.4 percent of daily fantasy baseball teams hit on the top-scoring player who was in 10 percent or fewer lineups. That's pretty remarkable.

At the other end of the spectrum, you can see there's a jump in the frequency of lineups with the best player who was 51-plus percent owned. That might be due to a larger player pool, but since not many players are ever in more than half of lineups, it could also be evidence to not forgo elite values. When a player stands out as the clear-cut top value, use him, regardless of the league type. It's the second-tier values you might want to fade in favor of less-utilized players.

NFL Passing Efficiency by Temperature

I've mentioned the importance of checking the weather in baseball on numerous occasions, namely because baseball games get rained out often. That doesn't happen in the NFL, but checking the weather is still important, especially late in the season.

To show why this is the case, I charted the effect that temperature (at kickoff) has on passing production.

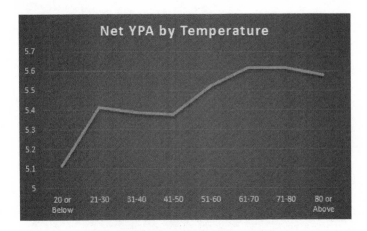

There's a pretty linear relationship here, with a very obvious drop when the temperature dips to around 20 degrees or below. That doesn't mean that a quarterback is fine if it's 21 degrees and doomed at 20 degrees, obviously—there's more of a range of efficiency—but the point is that very cold temperatures can have a significant effect on passing totals.

NFL Passing Efficiency by Wind Speed

It seems like many fantasy players care a whole lot about cold weather, but not nearly as much about a factor that I consider to be the most detrimental to the passing game: heavy winds. In windy games, quarterbacks have an extremely difficult time chucking the ball around.

But how windy is "too" windy?

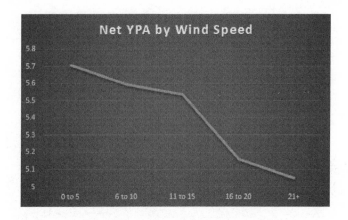

In terms of efficiency, there's a very obvious inverse relationship between wind speed and net YPA. Quarterbacks who have participated in games with winds between 16 to 20 MPH, for example, have been 15.0 percent less efficient than those playing in winds between 11 to 15 MPH.

Again, there's no distinct point at which a player becomes unusable, but once you start to approach 20 MPH, you really need to consider bypassing players in that game, especially those like DeSean Jackson or Mike Wallace who might be more dependent on throws that travel a long distance in the air.

In addition to reduced passing efficiency, here's another reason you might want to fade quarterbacks and pass-catchers in windy games.

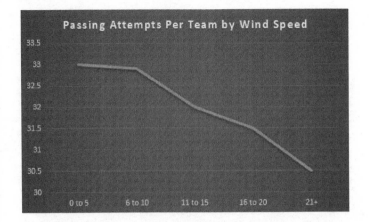

Not only does the wind dramatically affect passing efficiency, but coaches also adjust their game plans accordingly. The average quarterback will throw around 2.5 more passes in a dome than in 21-plus MPH winds.

Using these numbers, we can calculate the average dip in total passing yards to expect in certain situations based on wind speed. Quarterbacks typically produce right around 82 percent of their non-wind production in 21-plus MPH winds, for example.

A quarterback who averages, say, 275 yards in a dome would produce an average of just 225.5 passing yards per game in heavy winds. The reduced efficiency would also affect his touchdown total and of course the stats for all of his receivers as well.

The largest dip seems to some as the wind speed gets into the double-digits. Until you see winds around 10 MPH or faster, you can probably just project all quarterbacks and receivers as normal. As wind speed approaches 20 MPH, avoid quarterbacks and pass-catchers at all costs.

"If you stop at general math, you're only going to make general math money."

-   *Snoop Dogg*

7 A Sample from *How to Cash in on the Future of the Game*

The following is part of my chapter on bankroll management from Fantasy Football for Smart People: How to Cash in on the Future of the Game.

> *"No matter how good you are, you're going to lose one-third of your games. No matter how bad you are, you're going to win one-third of your games. It's the other third that makes the difference."*
>
> *- Tommy Lasorda*

If you've ever searched for fantasy football advice, the term "LOCKS" (all capital letters, usually) has become part of your vocabulary. Like the sports betting guru who offers "cant-miss" picks, many fantasy sports "experts" suggest that certain players are sure things in a given week. Calvin Johnson facing the league's 29th-ranked pass defense—you can pretty much take 150 yards and two touchdowns to the bank, right?

One of the most important steps in becoming a fantasy football master is realizing that you're going to be wrong. You're going to be wrong *a lot*. In a game filled with some variance, your advantage over even a novice in a head-to-head weekly matchup might be, say, 2-to-1, i.e. you're still going to lose 33 percent of the time.

Since the NFL is ruled by probabilities, even a perfect fantasy owner will lose. It's vital to understand that even if you're the world's premiere fantasy owner, you're not infallible. Just as a professional poker player can lose multiple hands in a row to a novice, so too can a pro lose to an amateur.

The same misunderstanding of probability that leads some to claim (and sometimes really believe) that their picks are fail-safe also often results in poor money management. After all, if you're entering leagues as if you're a 70 percent long-term winner when you're really no better than a coin flip, that's going to lead to an empty bankroll.

Thus, the percentage of your bankroll you place on each team should be a reflection of, among other things, your expected winning percentage.

Understanding Bankroll

Since your total bankroll will be the primary factor in determining how much you can put down in a given league, it's important that the amount of money you use in your calculations is your *true* bankroll, i.e. the maximum amount of money you're *willing to lose* playing the game. If you put $1,000 into your daily fantasy sports account but plan to remove the funds if you hit a certain low point, your true bankroll is $1,000 minus your low limit. If you calculate your entries as a function of the $1,000, they'll be too high and you'll be more likely to go bankrupt. Similarly, if you plan to add more funds to your account, formulating your buy-ins with a perceived $1,000 bankroll will potentially lead to lost profits.

Imagine a magical fantasy football genie has come to you and offered an enticing proposition: a guaranteed 80 percent winning percentage in daily fantasy football. Um, sign me up. The offer comes with one caveat, though; you must place 25 percent of your original bankroll on each lineup, and you need to participate in a minimum of 500 leagues. Do you take the offer?

While an 80 percent winning percentage is likely unattainable over the long-run even for an expert player, there's still no way you can take the genie's offer. Even with just a 20 percent chance of losing a game, it's going to happen. And occasionally, it will happen twice in a row. And once in a while, you'll lose three consecutive games. And, wait for it. . .over any four-game stretch (even with an incredible 80 percent expectation), you actually have a 0.16 percent chance of losing all four games—as in once in every 625 games, on average.

Would you go broke after the first four games? Probably not. But would it eventually happen? Yes. You're basically playing Russian roulette with your bankroll when, if your goal is long-term profitability, you should take chance out of the equation as much as possible. Now consider that a more realistic expected long-term winning percentage of 60 percent would result in four straight losses at *16 times the rate* of an 80 percent winning percentage, and you can see how money management starts to become the backbone of your daily fantasy football strategy.

How much is too much?

There are all sorts of theories regarding how much of your bankroll you should spend on each lineup. How should your expected return affect your entries? How about the number of players in a league? These questions haven't really been answered as it relates to daily fantasy football.

When fielding multiple fantasy lineups, the results are inherently tied to one another. You might start one player on multiple teams, for example, or you might start a quarterback and wide receiver duo. You could have the No. 1 receiver on his respective team on one of your squads and the No. 2 receiver on a different one. The dependent nature of your fantasy lineups makes them somewhat volatile, i.e. it would typically be unintelligent to enter with as much money as you would put down on independent events.

On top of that, your expected winning percentage won't be 60 percent if you enter anything other than head-to-head or 50/50 leagues. If you plan to enter a 100-team league that pays out the top 10 teams, for example, you probably can't expect to win money much more than 15 to 20 percent of the time, regardless of your skills.

Your Maximum Investment: The Ultimate Formula

Whether you play daily fantasy football for fun or for profit, you're presumably going to field more than one lineup. The number of teams you create and how you structure them will depend on your willingness to take on risk. Nonetheless, there are some basic parameters to follow when deciding upon your optimal investment for each lineup.

In playing daily fantasy football, I devised the following formula to determine the optimal amount to play on each lineup.

- **[(Percentage of owners who won't win)/6)]*(Expected winning percentage)*(Bankroll)**

Let's take an example. Suppose your bankroll is $1,000 and you want to enter a three-team league. To determine the optimal amount to enter, you'd first need to figure out the percentage of players that wouldn't win any money in the league. In a typical three-man league, only one person wins, meaning 67 percent of the owners would lose their investment.

Thus, the percentage of players who wouldn't win would be marked as "0.67." After dividing that number by 6, you'd multiply the result (0.11167) by your expected winning percentage in such a league. It is crucial that you don't overestimate your probability of winning. Actually, unless you have an established track record of success, you should estimate your chances of winning as the same as if the league were complete luck. In a three-man league, that would be 33 percent, or 0.33.

After multiplying 0.11167 by 33 percent to obtain 0.03685, you'll multiply that final number by the amount of your bankroll ($1,000). The proper amount to enter for someone in a three-team league that pays out one person is 3.685 percent, or $36.85.

Note that as you alter your expected winning percentage, the amount you should play changes as well. If you were confident you could take down 45 percent of three-man leagues, for example, your optimal entry amount (which is the total amount placed on each lineup, regardless of how you split it up among leagues) would increase to $50.25.

Using such a method, you can change the amount you place on your best lineups. If you use three head-to-head lineups and estimate your expected winning percentage to be 65 percent for the best combination of players and 55 percent for the worst, your ideal cash in play for each lineup with a $1,000 bankroll would gradually decline from $54.16 to $45.83.

Further, you can see how leagues with a low payout percentage subsequently lower the amount you should play. If you're in a 100-man league that pays out just 10 percent of owners, for example, your optimal entry with a bankroll of $1,000 would shrink to only $20.00.

Postface

"A postface is the opposite of a preface, a brief article or explanatory information placed at the end of a book. Postfaces are used in books so that the non-pertinent information will appear at the end of the literary work, and not confuse the reader.

There are at least two authentic examples of postfaces in published works. One can be found in the 1954 book Dalí's Mustache: A Photographic Interview, by Salvador Dali and Philippe Halsman. Another occurs in the philosopher Martin Heidegger's essay The Origin of the Work of Art and is further cited in Jacques Derrida's reading of it in The Truth in Painting (1987)."

Just Googled "opposite of preface" and this is what I got. Now I have a postface. Only the third authentic piece of revolutionary literature with a postface, and just the top artist and philosopher of the 20th century as company. It's whatever. Not saying it's a huge deal, but it's a huge deal.

So what should I include here? Well, it's my postface, so I guess the first thing I'll do is be selfish and tell you to buy my other books and visit my site FantasyFootballDrafting.com for updates from me. I post a lot of my content there, and I also sell various season-long and daily packages that you might (will) enjoy.

I'll just wait until you've bought my other stuff before I continue. Don't forget to hit submit. Get the overnight shipping, too. Okay, done with that?

Now, I'll be a little less selfish and tell you who was instrumental in the creation of this book: 4for4, RotoGrinders, RotoWire, and FantasyPros—all awesome sources of fantasy sports info and data. Daily fantasy experts CSURAM88, Mike5754, naapstermaan, headchopper, Notorious, and stlcardinals84—all among the very top daily fantasy players in the world. Jessica and Bowie—both among my favorite humans and dogs on the planet. My brothers, Uncle Bruce, Grandma and Grandpa, and parents—all of whom listen to me discuss daily fantasy sports on the phone, each and every day, without complaining all that much. And my friends Shoey, Tyler, TJ, and Nick—all of whom are weird.

And of course a huge thank you to DraftKings. When I approached them about this book, I told them that I think it could be wildly popular and useful if daily fantasy players could have access to their data. Their team worked their asses off—mining all that data isn't as simple as pushing a button—and they provided me with some awesome, unique stuff that I think will be extremely useful to you. There's no other daily site out there that's released data like this, and it's going to give you a leg up on the competition.

Thank you so much for reading. Don't forget that DraftKings is extending a special offer to readers of this book for a ridiculous 100 percent deposit bonus. Just visit DraftKings.com/Bales to sign up. Deposit $500, get $500 for free. Sweet.

Made in the USA
Lexington, KY
28 November 2015